Praise for WOMEN  KIDS

"I have read countless books on the subject of chosen childlessness, and I can't remember encountering one written with such candor, care, and precision of thought. It's easy to be glib about this subject, to tuck into defensiveness even while espousing pride and certainty. In *Women Without Kids*, Ruby Warrington does just the opposite. She tells her story with deep insight, great humor, and, best of all, an endless curiosity about the motives of her own mind. She's also done her research and knows her history, which she uses to draw important connections between the personal choices we make and the political and social landscapes that inform them. Essential reading no matter how you feel about kids!"

MEGHAN DAUM
editor of *Selfish, Shallow, and Self-Absorbed: Sixteen Writers on the Decision Not to Have Kids*

"*Women Without Kids* is a necessary invitation for us to reconsider our relationship to and with motherhood. Traditionally, being a child-free woman is expected to come with shame and regret—Ruby's latest work adds celebration and necessary nuance to the story of women and people of all genders intentionally living child-free."

RACHEL CARGLE
founder of The Loveland Foundation, The Loveland Group, and Rich Auntie Supreme

"In *Women Without Kids*, Ruby Warrington offers a compassionate exploration into what can be a highly loaded and emotional topic—the choice whether or not to have children. She explores the different factors that contribute to this decision, while her honest and vulnerable sharing of her personal journey inspires deep self-reflection in readers. *Women Without Kids* is a must-read for anyone seeking a full understanding of all the dynamics that play into this significant life choice."

DR. NICOLE LEPERA
New York Times bestselling author of *How to Do the Work*

"A radical, empathic, and provocative book that applies a feminist lens to what it means to be a woman without children in the twenty-first century. Through personal narrative and meticulous sociocultural research, Warrington demonstrates how consciously owning the experience of non-motherhood (whether or not by choice) has the potential to transform the experience of all women, mothers included, and to create a better world for all the generations that follow us."

JODY DAY
founder of Gateway Women, psychotherapist, and author of *Living the Life Unexpected: How to Find Hope, Meaning, and a Fulfilling Future Without Children*

"This isn't a book about not having kids for the defiantly childless. This is a book about motherhood under patriarchy—about our mothers, becoming mothers, not becoming mothers, choices and non-choices, and consequences and the things that separate us and keep us chained to a toxic cultural heritage. It is a startling, confronting, and liberating treatise."

HOLLY WHITAKER
New York Times bestselling author of *Quit Like a Woman*

"A sharp and intricate look at the personal and political sides of being a child-free woman. While reading, I was reminded of the first time I read Rebecca Solnit's *Men Explain Things to Me*—this is an exciting, bold, feminist book that gives the child-free conversation the space it deserves."

EMMA GANNON
bestselling author of *Olive* and host of the *Ctrl Alt Delete* podcast

"This is a wonderful book, personal yet universal, showing that what counts is not biological motherhood but caring—and that putting care front and center in our lives and social policies is how we will create the world that children, and all of us, need and want."

RIANE EISLER
author of *The Chalice and the Blade* and *The Real Wealth of Nations*, coauthor of *Nurturing Our Humanity*

"*Women Without Kids* makes a passionate and compelling case for rejecting old notions about the lives women should lead. True freedom is the right to forge unique paths—which won't always include motherhood. In tackling the antiquated stigmas surrounding childless women, Warrington is one of the trailblazers leading the way."

KIRSTEN MILLER
New York Times bestselling writer and author of *The Change*

Also by
Ruby Warrington

WOMEN
WITHOUT
KIDS

Also by
Ruby Warrington

Material Girl, Mystical World

Sober Curious

The Sober Curious Reset

WOMEN with out KIDS

THE REVOLUTIONARY RISE OF AN UNSUNG SISTERHOOD

RUBY WARRINGTON

sounds true
BOULDER, COLORADO

Sounds True
Boulder, CO

Published 2023, 2024

Book design by Charli Barnes

Printed in the United States of America

BK07045
978-1-64963-308-8

The Library of Congress has cataloged the hardcover edition as follows:

Names: Warrington, Ruby, author.
Title: Women without kids : the revolutionary rise of an unsung sisterhood
  / Ruby Warrington.
Description: Boulder, CO : Sounds True, 2023.
Identifiers: LCCN 2022040417 (print) | LCCN 2022040418 (ebook) | ISBN
  9781683649274 (hardback) | ISBN 9781683649281 (ebook)
Subjects: LCSH: Childfree choice. | Women—Psychology.
Classification: LCC HQ755.8 .W377 2023 (print) | LCC
HQ755.8 (ebook) |
  DDC 306.872082—dc23/eng/20220826
LC record available at https://lccn.loc.gov/2022040417
LC ebook record available at https://lccn.loc.gov
/2022040418

For my family

Contents

Sisterhood of the Selfish Cunts

THERE'S A GAME I like to play sometimes when my mind is picking at the scabs of my self-esteem, looking for ways to prove what a loser I am. I call it *Does She Have Kids?* Okay, "game" is maybe stretching it. The only skill required is the ability to type the name of the woman in question into Wikipedia. "She" is invariably somebody who has impressed me with her talent, her vision, her moxie. I'll have been watching one of her movies, reading one of her books, or tracing a finger over her picture—smart, self-possessed, celebrated—in a magazine. She is around the same age as me—swimming somewhere in the shallows of midlife, sometimes older—and something about her demeanor, or the quality of her achievements, or how she looks at the camera like she owns the place, makes me question whether she is also a mother. *All this, and kids too?*

From the depths of my sofa, where my husband, my cat, and I bathe nightly in the hypnotic blue light of the TV, I reach for my phone, type in her name, and wait for Wikipedia to do its thing.

Maybe this time she'll surprise me. As soon as the page loads, my eyes scan the pale blue box that contains her basic biographical info. Birth date, Nationality, Occupation . . . Children. A single digit (usually it's a "1" or a "2," but in the case of Nancy Pelosi, a "5"!) confirms what the culture at large has led me to believe is true: that as a woman without kids, my life is incomplete. That as a female-bodied individual who has chosen not to reproduce, my own list of achievements will always come up short. That as a girl who never dreamed of baby names, or wondered who the dad would be, maybe there is even *something wrong with me*. I place my phone back on the coffee table, retrain my gaze on the TV. Yep, I lose. My game has reinforced the message once again: that as a woman without kids I am less-than, a failure, a freak.

But me not being a mother feels as fundamentally a part of me as the freckles on my face; not something I would ever have thought to question had it not become apparent that someday, being somebody's mom would be expected of me. An existence that revolved around the changing of diapers, the sleepless nights, and the frantic, awkward *school run*, my predetermined destiny, based on the double X chromosomes at the center of my being. Hours, days, and eventually years of my own freedom and deep thinking, put on hold while tending to the shaping and nurturing of young minds.

Is this how Wikipedia woman sees her life? When I picture her with her kids, the scene looks nothing like my own childhood. Instead, I see an idealized version of motherhood that I, as with all women, am supposed to want to aspire to. They are gathered in a spacious kitchen, the light from large windows (a skylight?) spilling over crayon drawings and unfinished homework, cold chewy bits of half-eaten toast. They are laughing, and then someone is crying, and there are hugs and kisses to make it all feel better. She is responding to emails on her phone with one hand, balancing a small, warm, wriggling body on her hip with the other, absorbing the oxytocin from her child's embrace like it's just another sup-plement she takes with her morning coffee. Flash-forward. The kids, fully grown, are home for the holidays. Tall, strong, and full of tales, helping themselves to beers from the fridge, they occupy the kitchen with opinions she realizes she has helped to shape. I grew you, she thinks to herself, held snug as heavy cashmere by the satisfaction of a job well done. What fulfillment. What private *riches*. Whatever accolades she has amassed, whatever other *stuff* she's done with her life, it has all been for this, for *them*.

THUD-a-duh-da-THUD-a-duh-da. The sound of helicopter blades swiping at the night sky filling the windows of my Brooklyn apartment breaks my reverie. Outside, the streets thrum with the restless energy of a million dreams destined never to come true; but in here, for now, all is peaceful, quiet, safe. One wall lined with rows of color-coordinated books, each having taught me something profound about the world and my place in it. Every framed photograph and piece of artwork telling its own story about the adventures I have lived. The laptop on the table behind me, a portable office, portfolio, and artist's studio all in one, an entire career encased in scratched matte silver aluminum. Another device, my phone, a mystical technological amulet teeming with connections to family, friends, and colleagues, connecting me to the world around me with a steady drip of headlines, information, and ideas. And beside me on the sofa, S, my husband and best friend of twenty-three years, a person I never expected or tried to find, and who has wound up being both my biggest cheerleader and my most honest mirror for more than half my life.

Taking it all in soothes me. Nothing is missing; everything is in its place. A life designed to fit me like a second skin. A life that is full to the brim. I shift position on the sofa, sitting up straight and bending one tracksuit-panted leg into half-lotus. Deep breath. Once the wave of insecurity has washed through me, I reconsider why I need to know—*all this, and a mother, too?*

The truth revealing itself with each discrete, internal fist-pump when I find another one of me, *of us*. What I'm really looking for is other *women without kids*.

* * *

Because we're everywhere, aren't we? Amid the cacophony of our chaotic arrival in the new millennium, motherhood is still upheld as every woman's rightful, natural role, the path to her ultimate fulfillment. And yet, more and more of us are either questioning whether the vocation of childrearing is for us, or opting out full stop. As it stands, almost half of all women in the United States do not have kids, while fertility issues, the cost of raising a kid, and concerns about the environment are other factors contributing to the birthrate having hit a historic low in the summer of 2020.[1] Meanwhile, the world population is forecasted to peak in 2064, with twenty-three countries seeing populations shrink *by more than 50 percent by 2100*.[2] For some of us, non-motherhood is a conscious choice; for others, it just hasn't happened. But regardless of our reasons, the writing is smeared across the wall in brick red menstrual blood: within this stealth withdrawal from our reproductive duties lies the makings of a movement. And if you're reading this, you're already part of it.

But where are we? Not only are women without kids underrepresented in the mainstream media, we are still seen as the anomaly. At best, a woman who is not also a mother is a strange bird, faulty goods. If she *can't* have kids she is often portrayed as sad and damaged ("Such a shame"); if she simply *won't* (rarely is it that straightforward) she is either deluded, destined to regret it, or written off as cold-hearted, narcissistic, and career-obsessed. What a *selfish cunt*.

Please don't be offended by my salty language there! *Selfish Cunt* was going to be the title of this book; it filled my frontal cortext with vibrating neon letters the instant I considered writing on this subject. The notion that it is *selfish* not to dedicate one's life to the birthing, nurturing, and raising of one's children being the ultimate indictment against women without kids. But realistically, with the word *cunt* being practically unprintable, as a title it was never going to fly. Which is the other reason I like it; both "selfish" and "cunt" are ripe for reclamation when it comes to matters of women's self-sovereignty and bodily autonomy. Which hints at some of the core themes we will be discussing here.

Honestly? It's always pissed me off that the *worst word* you can call a person is also a name for the most sacred, most violated, most politicized, and most policed part of the female body. After all, it is only relatively recently, in the grand and grisly scheme of things, that women have even had the option not to bear children, our cunts not been regarded as the property of either our husbands or the state. An option that remains off-limits, still, for millions; women for whom there exists, in the words of British advice columnist Mariella Frostrup, "a straight line between puberty, marriage, sex and motherhood that continues on a loop until you die of exhaustion or reach menopause and breathe a sigh of relief."[3]

In developed, democratic nations, we like to think that we have come a long way in terms of women's rights to autonomy and self-authorship. Undoubtedly, this is the case. So why is it then that being a woman without kids is still so taboo? Why is the path to non-motherhood still subject to so much stigma, shame, and othering? Why are so many women still corralled into motherhood against their will (literally, with the 2022 overturning of *Roe v. Wade* in the United States)? And why are so many others struggling to afford to have kids, experiencing fertility issues that mean they can't get pregnant, or leaving it until "too late"? Above all, why is there so little discussion or understanding of the personal and societal factors that inform our procreative outcomes—factors that unite what I have come to see as the *unsung sisterhood* of women without kids?

The question—*Why don't you want to be a mom?*—used to annoy the hell out of me, the implication being that I definitely *should*. Most of the time, one answer had always been enough for me: *I just don't*. But on darker days, my lack of a discernable maternal instinct manifested in murky feelings of inadequacy and self-doubt. *Surely, there must be something wrong with me*. A creeping suspicion that spiked during my thirties, while I was working as a magazine journalist in London. I was asked by several editors to write about my "unorthodox" stance. Behind my back (it not being considered polite to ask outright), my best friend also had to field the question: *Why, oh WHY, does she not want kids?* In response, I jotted off articles explaining that, for now, I wanted to focus on my career, and that my life already felt complete.

But eventually, the intense scrutiny made me question whether there wasn't more to this story. After all, it was sort of *odd* not to want a child; wasn't the procreation of the species the reason we were here? But the really odd thing, it began to seem to me, was that all women were expected to revel in the role of mother, despite major discrepancies in our personalities, our ambitions, our material resources, and our mental and emotional well-being. And why was it that my other desires for my life were not seen as equally valid? Why *was* the cost of raising a child so steep? Why was the love I felt for my husband and my friends not the same as the "real" love I was told I would feel for my child? And if my choice *did* make me selfish and neurotic, then what was the root of these neuroses?

In many ways, this book began as a deep dive into my experience of making peace with all of this. In the first instance, I hope that reading it will help to do the same for you. As I began to join the dots, I had come to see that me being a woman without kids did not make me a freak: it made a lot of sense. That in some ways, it was also the natural outcome of a confluence of factors that have shaped all of our lives, for better and for worse, over the course of centuries. For so long, motherhood has been synonymous with womanhood—but in reality, there are many, many very valid reasons not to be a mom. And it was as I began to consider how I might present these findings that the scope of my new project began to widen.

I had always felt like I was the only one who didn't want to be a mom. But as I got deeper into my research, it became clear that I was no longer the anomaly. If the drop-off in the birthrate was due to the fact that the vast majority of women were having fewer kids, increasingly, it was because more of us were having none at all. If the question had always been "Why don't you want kids?" now I needed to know: *Why have WE stopped having kids?* Given that motherhood has long been considered the biological imperative of every person who is born a woman, something profound was evidently occurring in the evolution of womankind.

I began working on my hypothesis for what this might be against the backdrop of the COVID-19 pandemic. It was the summer when used pizza boxes emblazoned with the words "Black Lives Matter" adorned the windows of luxury Williamsburg condos and trans activists canceled Harry Potter. Thousands of miles to the north, as we all hunkered down and girded ourselves against apocalypse, the last intact ice shelf in the Canadian arctic, a slab of frigid gray ecology larger than Manhattan, finally broke free and shattered.[4] From where my research was taking me, it was as if the social justice and environmentalist movements, coupled with the social and economic fallout from centuries of extractive capitalism, had created the perfect storm. Almost overnight, not having kids was no longer being seen as a crime against humanity; it was beginning to emerge as its own kind of destiny.

* * *

But before we go there, a few words on who this book is for. Given that the story of my development from girl, to woman, to non-mother forms the backbone of this text, it is likely that those readers who have either chosen not to become a mom or who are still grappling with that choice will find themselves reflected most clearly in these pages. But in the writing of it, I have uncovered common threads that I believe will be relatable for anybody who identifies as a woman without kids.

As such, I am speaking to the ones who've never wanted to be mothers, the ones who are teetering on the fence, the ones who've tried and failed to become parents, and the ones for whom it just never happened. This book is for the ones who don't have wombs and who feel anything but barren. It is for those for whom health issues or other disabilities have blocked the path to parenthood. It is for anybody whose sexual orientation or gender expression has written them out of the heteronormative story about what it means to "start a family." And it is even for those moms who may have found themselves, in the flat, scooped-out quiet of the 3 am feed, questioning where the fuck their minds, their identities, their *lives* have gone. The ones who sometimes— whisper it—*wish they didn't have kids.*

We selfish cunts come in all shapes and sizes. If you really want to know *What's the story there?* you will find our narratives to be as diverse and as richly textured as the undergrowth that carpets an ancient, forgotten forest. We all have our reasons for being (or wanting to be) nobody's mom; some dark and spiky, others green and luscious. But popular terminology for women without kids neatly sorts the ones who *can't* from the ones who *won't.* Within this binary, we are either sadly "childless" or defiantly "childfree," the latter often seen as selfish and deviant, and the former as deserving of our utmost sympathy. When in reality, our stories are awash with nuance.

But I also acknowledge that not everything I have to say will be for everyone. I cannot know how it feels to grieve lost dreams of becoming a mom—even if completing this manuscript has found me grieving other things. In addition, I realize that me not wanting to have kids is its own form of privilege; it is far easier to opt out of motherhood than to want to have a child when this is not an option for you. This in addition to me having been born with all the benefits that accrue to a white, heterosexual, cis-gendered, able-bodied, college-educated, British woman. If anything, not having kids has made it even easier for me to partake of the opportunities therein—not least because not being a mother makes me *more like a man*. A definite advantage in a world built by men, for men.

On the subject of privilege, please let it also be clear that every one of the structural issues impacting women's reproductive outcomes that I cover here disproportionately impacts women of color.[5] From a history of forced sterilizations, to the Black maternal health crisis, to a simple lack of access to resources, race adds another layer of complexity to the question of whether or not to become a mom.[6]

And yet every woman without kids, regardless of our circumstances, will have been subject to similar stigmas and prejudices about the fact we are not mothers. Will have grappled with similar feelings of shame, otherness, and self-doubt. Will have mopped up the pity, envy, disappointment, and judgment that is often projected onto us from family, friends, colleagues, and the wider culture, about this most intensely personal of circumstances.

Like, where does *that* shit come from? This is seriously toxic stuff—and it prevents us from having honest, vulnerable, and multifaceted conversations about the forces that have shaped the women that we are. According to Jody Day, founder of Gateway

Women, an organization for the involuntarily childless, it all has the same rotten root: pronatalism. The ideology, that is, that says "parents are more important than non-parents, and that families are more respectable and more valid than single people."

You have felt the influence of this, right? One of the corner-stones of heteropatriarchy, pronatalism insists that the *reason we are here* is to couple-up and procreate. This belief is so embedded in societies across the globe that it operates like a microchip in our brains, coding feelings, thoughts, and beliefs before we have a chance to question them. Pronatalism is what tells us that it is selfish and narcissistic not to have kids. Pronatalism is what makes women feel like they have "failed" when they can't get pregnant. Pronatalism is what denounces queer sex, and all non-procreative sex, as "perverse." Pronatalism is what turns up the volume on our biological clocks; what gives other people permission to nose into our private business; and what gives politicians a say about what we do with our wombs.

Pronatalism is also the reason there is still no specific, widely used terminology that validates the life-path of women without kids: we are *non*-mothers, women *without* kids, either child-*less* or child-*free*, all of which emphasize the absence of a child. Even "nullipara," the medical term for a person who has never carried a live birth to term, has its root in the Latin *nullus*, "none," and *para*, from *parere*, "bear children."

And pronatalism is behind what I have termed the Mommy Binary. That is, the false divide that exists between moms and non-moms, the childless and the childfree—forever pitting us against each other in toxic cycles of compare and despair. Two things I want us to take as universal? First, the fact that every woman, and every human being, is entitled to self-determine when it comes to our procreative potential. And second, that if being women without kids marks us as different, then good—because womankind needs *different*.

We need for there to be zero pressure for anybody to become a parent if for any reason they do not want kids or are otherwise unable to perform this role. We need more women channeling more time, energy, and other resources into other activities besides childrearing. We need more resources being put into the human beings that already exist! We also need a recognition that goes beyond lip service of how fucking hard it is sometimes to be a mom. We need to see that this is not a personal failing on the part of any one individual—but that it represents a collective failure to support women properly in their mothering. And perhaps above all else, we need a serious conversation about the planet we are leaving behind for the kids—even if they're not our kids.

* * *

Which begins to get under the skin of where this project has taken me, the farther-reaching themes that move below the surface of this subject having pulled me down and under, to places that I didn't even know that we would need to go. To be clear (if it wasn't already clear): this is NOT a book about how to live a fabulous childfree life. If anything, the writing process has been shockingly confronting. And if some of what you uncover in the reading makes you as uncomfortable as it has made me, then also good: meeting ourselves at our edges is how we live beyond the stereotypes and clichés that keep us playing out tired old stories on repeat. The one about a woman's rightful, *natural* role, being that of nurturing caretaker, being long overdue a rewrite.

This has already been happening online. During the decade since I was first asked to write about not having kids, a new guard of young women writers has begun populating a freshly digitized and democratized media landscape with blogs, op-eds, and

TikTok skits on their ambivalence about motherhood: Working *and* being a mom looks really hard. And who can afford the childcare anyway? Motherhood is mind-numbing and unfulfilling. I'm freezing my eggs *now* so I don't have to think about it.

From where I'm standing, it is becoming clear that we are in the midst of a subtle yet tectonic shift. For so long, becoming a mother has been the only option for women; suddenly, for some, it feels like it is not an option at all. A shift that reminds me of the famous Ernest Hemingway quote: "How did you go bankrupt? Two ways. Gradually, then suddenly."

But are we going bankrupt? Sometimes people talk about the drop-off in the birth rate as if we are witnessing the end of humanity as we know it, with women without kids being held personally responsible for this. But what if the revolutionary rise of our unsung sisterhood is in fact heralding the start of a new chapter in our human story? One that holds the potential for exponential healing—individually, for our societies, for our planet, and on behalf of our ancestry?

In some ways, women without kids are the canaries in the coal mine: our very existence is symbolic of the fact that current conditions on planet Earth are simply not conducive to childrearing and family life. To the thriving of humanity, period. Viewed another way, we are representative of a rapidly evolving legacy for womankind, and of the dismantling of patriarchal values that grant women only one place in society—the home. As such, our movement can be read as equal parts self-preservation, empowerment, and birth strike. Not having kids is not a political statement; it is a deeply personal orientation. But motherhood being so politicized, the revolutionary rise of women without kids also can't *not* be part of a wider conversation about gender, sexuality, family, and equality.

For example, if we are seen as "selfish," then isn't this because we are still not used to women having the ultimate say about what we do with our bodies, our money, and our lives? If we are "neurotic," isn't it because many of us have grown up in societies where women and woman-identifying individuals are simultaneously "empowered" and objectified? And if our very existence strikes fear and loathing in the hearts of conservative politicians, isn't this because pregnancy and childrearing are where the buck stops when it comes to the patriarchal order of the gendered status quo?

I will also be asking us to consider, deeply, the Big Picture questions posed by the global reproduction slowdown here. Like, what if more women having more time, energy, and other resources at our disposal means more women leaders in business, politics, and the arts? What if not all of us are supposed to have kids, and what if this were considered the norm? What would it mean to focus on our individual and collective healing, before we throw any new humans into the mix? What would it really look like to heal our relationship to the universal mother, Earth? And the biggest one of all: *Is the meaning of life really only to create more life?*

I don't have the answers to these questions; I don't think anybody does. But that doesn't mean they're not worth asking. For my part, I have done this with the help of the writers, philosophers, and healers I have interviewed along the way, interviews that I have also recorded as a *Women Without Kids* podcast series to accompany this book. Countless articles, research papers, and other texts have also helped to inform the ideas and arguments I introduce. In my personal life, I have engaged in deep and searching conversations with the women I know about our experiences of mothering and being mothered, and I encourage you to do the same as you encounter whatever comes up as you read along.

And finally, in order to widen my circle of influence, I also conducted an online survey to garner further insights into the diverse lives and experiences of women without kids. The 160 people who responded range in age from twenty-four to seventy-four and represent a range of ethnicities and socioeconomic backgrounds. Some are married, some are single, some are straight, and some are queer. All identify as "women without kids," and they each have their individual reasons for this. Their testimonies floored me with their vulnerability and their generosity, and I have included select outtakes throughout.

What I hope to show in these pages is that every woman who challenges the conventions of motherhood is a force for change, both individual and collective. Not because of the things she does, but because of who she is. I want us to acknowledge that it is time for a reckoning with outmoded ideals about what it means to be a mother: to be a woman, period. Rather than a dystopian denial of life itself, I want to present a radical reframing of what it really means not to be a mom—and for us to see ourselves as the torchbearers of an alternative vision for a fully self-actualized womankind.

Along the way, I would like you to imagine with me a world where our legacy is up for grabs, our place in history waiting to be written. A world where no woman is required to birth a child in order for her to validate her existence. I want to remind you that being a mother is neither the be-all-and-end-all nor the icing on the cake, and that any and all expressions of a person's procreative potential are equally, vitally valid. That whatever your reason for being nobody's mom, or even a *selfish cunt*, there is nothing wrong with you, and you are not the only one. Above all, I want us to be united, in sisterhood, as women without kids.

"

"I didn't have the patience (for parenthood), and I didn't want to devote all my time to raising kids. I had other interests I preferred to pursue."

— age sixty-seven, single

"I am from Poland, where the traditional family model is still very strong. But I never had any 'maternal feelings.' When my older sister had a son, she asked me to babysit him when he was six months old. Those were the longest five hours of my life, and I couldn't wait to give the child back to his mother."

— age thirty-eight, in a partnership

"I always 'knew' I would have kids. Daydreamed. Decided on all the names I liked. Wanted three. And then one day I realized that I was terrified to have children and the only reason I was doing any of that planning was because I didn't think I had a choice."

— age thirty, in a new relationship

"

CHAPTER 1

The Motherhood Spectrum

THE WAITING ROOM at the therapist's office was quiet and dark and was filled with creaky furniture that had seen better, happier days. Located behind a heavy wooden door in East London's Spitalfields, *Jack the Ripper territory*, I had chosen the place because it was walking distance from work. As I waited, I chewed on the waxy skin at the edges of my nail beds and refreshed the needy stream of emails on my BlackBerry. At age thirty-four, my career was going places. But it was the relentless, deadline-heavy pressure of my magazine job, coupled with something indefinably . . . *not right*, a constant hum of nervous energy, the sense that my cover was about to be blown at any moment, of everything being lost and my becoming destitute overnight, that had brought me here, reluctantly, this muggy Tuesday lunchtime.

The therapist had thin blond hair and the yellowed, papery skin of a lifelong smoker. It was our first session, and she started by assessing the lay of the land. What had brought me here? ("Just this constant anxiety. I often find myself either crying or feeling really angry for no reason.") How was my relationship with my parents? ("I don't see them very often. My mum and I aren't that close, and my dad has another family now.") Was I married? ("Yes, my husband is my best friend. I can't imagine ever not liking him.") And did I have children of my own? ("No. I've never wanted to have kids.") She stopped, pen poised above her notepad, as she shifted in her chair and changed the cross of her legs. Her pause so thick with intent you could bite into it. *And why was that, did I think?*

There it was, less than fifteen minutes into our session, the gazillion-dollar question. One I had fielded on repeat since I had failed to grow out of my childhood aversion to babies. My answer always the same: *I've just never felt . . . the urge?* Because that was what happened, wasn't it? By the time I'd reached my thirties it seemed to me that every woman, everywhere, at a certain point in her life, seemed to decide that nothing else mattered as much as becoming a mom. But never having experienced for myself the onset of *baby fever*—the intense, life-affirming desire to birth and nurse a child of my own—I had only the accounts of the other women in my life to go by. Them, and the celebrities who gushed in the pages of the magazine where I worked: you could forget the accolades and the creative freedom, they insisted, it was having a child that had finally made them feel complete. I could see why my nonplussed attitude to motherhood confused people; the maternal instinct had to be some holy hormonal shit.

But while my lack of desire to become a mom marked me out as *different*, it still wasn't something I'd paid that much attention to. I suppose I figured that the baby fever would kick in at some point, and then I'd see where I was at with it. But the therapist seemed to think that she was onto something. The clock tick-tocked, and the silence between us stretched like gum about to snap. "Let's stay with that," she said. "You're the age most women are planning a family. Why is that not appealing to you?" I squirmed in my own cracked leather seat, my irritation like a swarm of ants surging across my back and up between my shoulder blades. *Really?* Deep intake of breath. *We were going to make this about my fucking biology?*

I had expected her to ask about my family. They fuck you up, your mum and dad, and all of that. But I came here to talk about the constant pressure I put on myself; the feeling that nothing I did, or achieved, would ever be enough. I wanted her to ask me why I drank so much. I was ready, finally, to talk about why I stayed with my abusive ex for so long, and the lasting impact of that relationship. But instead of voicing any of this, I smiled politely like the nice girl that I was and gave a little shrug. "It's just never been a priority for me." By the time the session dragged to its awkward conclusion, she told me we'd come back to the kids thing next week. I left and headed back to the glossy hubbub of the magazine office with my nerves unsoothed, as tightly wound a trap of anxiety and self-doubt as when I went in.

* * *

It would be ten years before I tried therapy again. A decade during which the question—*Why don't you want kids?*—would continue to hound me. Prior to that point, not seeing myself as a mother had not felt like a problem; it just felt like me. Sure, the question had always been there; I knew that it was sort of odd not to want to procreate. But now it hung in the air of my existence like the intrusive perfume of the village gossip. I was "that age," after all, and as my biological clock began to count down the years, I started to give it more silent, persistent consideration than perhaps any other topic in my life. It surfaced each time a friend became pregnant. I discussed it with my husband, at length, whenever my period was more than two days late. And, over time, what had always felt like my most truthful answer—*I just don't want to be a mom*—began to bob about on a rising tide of doubts. Doubt that I would ever "grow up" or be taken seriously if I didn't have kids; whether I would ever be seen as a "real" woman. Doubt in my capacity to give and receive unconditional love. As noted in the introduction, so embedded in the culture was the notion that being a woman meant being a mom that I began to doubt whether there wasn't even something biologically wrong with me.

But gradually, a more expansive line of inquiry emerged. "Why don't I want kids?" became "Why am I expected to want to be a mom?" This is the question I want us to consider, in depth, together in this chapter. In my case, this reframe also opened up broader areas for consideration: Why are women told we'll regret it if we don't have kids? Why are we sometimes shamed for prioritizing other avenues to fulfillment? Why aren't men expected to want to be fathers? How is it that more and more women are leaving it until "too late"? Is it even ethical to bring a child into the world given the current climate emergency? And not least, thanks to the advent of the exhausted mommy blogger, sending an SOS into the ethers of the internet from the depths of her postpartum psychosis: *When did it get so fucking* hard *to be a mom?*

These are questions for which it seems obvious that there are no simple, one-size-fits-all answers. Questions that also led me to wonder: what if, rather than motherhood being every woman's natural, God-given role, some of us, regardless of our biology, are simply *more suited to the role and the vocation of parenthood than others?*

This brings me to a concept that I have termed the Motherhood Spectrum. In essence, this speaks to the idea that any individual person's desire and aptitude for parenthood will be influenced by a multitude of factors—everything from our basic personality, to our family and cultural background, to our desires and ambitions for our life, to our finances, to our physical and mental health, to our relationship status. It also does away with the notion that not being a mother, not wanting to be mom, or not naturally reveling in the role means that there is something wrong with us. Rather, it suggests that there is everything wrong with a society that treats biological women as a monolith—as if being born with a bloody c-word between your legs automatically equips a person for parenthood.

The concept of the Motherhood Spectrum solidified for me after I discovered a 1996 book by New York–based psychoanalyst (and woman without kids) Jeanne Safer, titled *Beyond Motherhood*. In the years since I first sat in that therapist's chair, and as I neared and cleared the hump of forty, the intensity with which I'd been confronted with other people's projections about my reproductive situation was matched only by the fervor with which those around me began to obsess about when to have kids, with whom (or not), and how much they were prepared to spend on IVF (in vitro fertilization) if that was how it went.

I picked up Safer's book in the midst of this commotion, and two sentences in particular cut through any confusion I might have been feeling as a result like a hot knife: "Motherhood is no longer a necessary nor a sufficient condition for maturity or fulfillment," she writes. "It is a biological potential and a psychological vocation which a significant minority of women, upon reflection, recognize does not suit them." And it is a minority that is becoming more significant with each new generation.

Reading Safer's words was like wiping the condensation from a steamed-up mirror and looking myself in the eyes. However, the fact that her book was published coming up on thirty years ago, and that it remains one of a handful of largely academic texts to probe more deeply into the psychological aspects of what is the most important and impactful decision of any woman's life, speaks volumes about the still revolutionary nature of what her statement implies: *that having kids is not "every woman's" natural, and therefore ultimately fulfilling, role and purpose.* And there I'd been attempting to pathologize my lack of a discernable maternal instinct. Closing my eyes tight, and trying to conjure a sensation, a desire, a yearning, that I had no point of reference for. Now, yet another question presented itself: what if this "instinct" I was supposed to embody was as much of a social and a psychological construct as it was a part and parcel of being born a biological woman?

After all, the fact that more and more people are questioning whether motherhood is for them suggests that the extent to which one experiences the maternal instinct is less to do with our hormones and more likely the result of a unique constellation of psychological, environmental, and even cosmic factors that shape our individual identities. Could it be, when it comes to nature versus nurture, that the influences we are exposed to might even have the greater say when it comes to our reproductive choices?

For example, each person of childbearing age today is impacted to some extent by practical concerns that are in many ways unique to early twenty-first-century life: the rising cost of raising a child, an increasingly competitive and unstable job market, lack of support from a wider family network, and the complexities of meeting a suitable coparent. For younger generations, eyes turned skyward to read foreboding smoke signals from the future of a planet on fire, fears about the climate catastrophe that is unfolding in every microsecond may be enough to have quashed any procreative "urges." For somebody for whom becoming a mom *just hasn't happened*, perhaps she's experienced some of the fertility issues that experts say are also connected to modern environmental factors. Or perhaps she has been too busy doing what have felt like other equally important and fulfilling things.

And then there are the intimately personal reasons, often imperceptible to the naked eye, that apply equally across all camps—and which may also impact how a woman feels about motherhood *after* she's had kids: a desire to focus on her career; a fear of childbirth; doubts about her childrearing abilities; trepidation around reliving her own difficult childhood; just not really seeing herself as a "mom."

All of which will help determine where a person may orient on the Motherhood Spectrum, and which are equally valid reasons for not wanting or having children. Take a minute and think about which of the above factors have had the most say over your feelings about becoming a mom. Maybe it's a combination of the above. What else comes up for you as you reflect on this?

When we then map the practical challenges of motherhood against the opportunities that have opened up to women over the past half century, the question many of us are asking is also less "Do I want to have kids?" and more "What are all the potential life-paths that I could pursue?" A question that women of previous generations *never even got to ask themselves in the first place*—and which, as we shall see, the revolutionary sisterhood of women without kids is poised to help normalize for all women to come.

As Jeanne Safer writes: "My decision never to bear children reflects my entire history, the interaction of temperament and circumstance, fear and desire, capacities and limitations, that makes me who I am." Pause again here, and consider: What are all the things that make you uniquely YOU, and how have these things influenced how you feel about being a woman without kids? For me, reflecting on this helped me feel more confident than ever about my "Affirmative No" about motherhood, the reasons for which will become clear as I share more of my story in the coming pages. This is also Safer's term—introduced in a follow-up essay to *Beyond Motherhood* that she penned for Meghan Daum's 2015 anthology *Selfish, Shallow, and Self-Absorbed: Sixteen Writers on the Decision Not to Have Kids*. Here, she explains that asserting an Affirmative No reframes the no as a positive: "It also often means saying 'yes' to points of view that may be unpopular but that are in fact authentically in line with your own thoughts and feelings." Further, she writes: "[An Affirmative No] is not an act of rebellion; it is an act of willed self-assertion, of standing your ground on your own behalf."

Which feels a lot more like my experience of rejecting motherhood, and quite a lot like how I have learned to approach life in general. Not least from my own mother, as we shall see. Meanwhile, it also makes sense that at the other end of the Motherhood Spectrum lies an "Affirmative Yes"; the full-body, soul-powered, solid-gold knowing that you *do* want to be a mom. Perhaps, for some, that this is even *the reason you are here*. But if these are the extremes, what about all those who fall somewhere in between?

Given the infinitely disparate factors that make us who we are and that dictate what we need to feel satisfied and content, I would argue that this is *most women*. Taking into account what we also know about the challenges of modern motherhood, coupled with the opportunities afforded us by wave after wave of feminist fight, it also seems perfectly normal, *natural* even, that a significant majority of women would experience a degree of ambivalence about signing on for the job. After all, anybody who's ever expressed doubts about getting knocked up will also have been told that "nobody ever feels ready to have kids"—which is often invoked to encourage potential parents to just go for it already. But I know plenty of people who have felt very, *very* ready to become parents, and like now is *exactly* the right time. People who have found themselves consumed with *baby fever*. And if some of us will always be more ready than others, doesn't it follow that some may never be ready at all?

Not to mention that the very real concept of "parental readiness" (which we'll also be discussing in depth elsewhere) is worthy of serious consideration when it comes to the future well-being of both mother and child. And yet, what's still held up as *normal and natural* is a woman's Affirmative Yes about being a mom—the notion that every woman, given the opportunity and the biological capacity, would gladly leap at the chance. So how did this binary view of motherhood—that it's either a natural, celebratory YES! or a selfish, dysfunctional NO—come to be? And what happens when we begin to acknowledge the nuance that exists in between?

* * *

As I touched on in the introduction, what I have termed the *Mommy Binary* has its roots in patriarchy and its offshoot: pronatalism. The origins of this go all the way back to the global transition from feudalism to capitalism during the fifteenth through eighteenth centuries—a period during which motherhood began to be seen as women's *only viable role in society*. Feminist scholar Silvia Federici paints a vivid picture of this historical shift in *Caliban and the Witch*—in which she posits that the very purpose of the witch hunts that accompanied this era, for example, was to put control of women's bodies and reproductive function into the hands of the newly minted owning class: wealthy white men, a.k.a. the founding fathers of patriarchy.

Said "witches" represented "a world of female subjects that capitalism had to destroy: the heretic, the healer, the disobedient wife, the woman who dared to live alone." Among them, many a woman without kids. Women in turn whose life choices went against the requirements of the developing capitalist machine, which demanded a continual source of fresh "labor-power" (i.e., people) in order to fulfill its mandate of perpetual growth. The acquisition of more human labor and other natural resources at the lowest possible cost to those in power also being the core driver of both colonization and slavery.

In her seminal *Of Woman Born: Motherhood as Experience and Institution*, Adrienne Rich draws a distinction between the act of mothering and the "patriarchal institution" of motherhood—the latter essentially reducing women's wombs to the "technologies of reproduction." Herein we see the original "objectification" of the female body. It was within this construct that the bearing and raising of children also began to be positioned as women's *biological imperative* (a message that is essentially unimpeachable: who can argue with nature?). In addition, Rich writes: "The regulation of women's reproductive power by men . . . the legal and technical control by men of contraception, fertility, abortion, obstetrics, gynecology, and extrauterine reproductive experiments—are all essential to the patriarchal system, *as is the negative or suspect status of women who are not mothers* (emphasis mine)."

And so we see the seeds of the Mommy Binary being sewn: the notion, that is, that mothers are "natural" and valid, and non-mothers are defective, an aberration. This is the kernel of the belief system that gives other people permission to talk about our procreative choices as if our wombs were public property. It is also the source of any shame and otherness that any of us here have ever felt about being women without kids.

As Federici writes, it was with the industrialization of the world that "women's [childrearing] labor began to appear as a natural resource, available to all, no less than the air we breathe or the water we drink." The implications of this were literal for enslaved African women, who were forced to procreate in order to replenish the labor force. Elsewhere, this dynamic was solidified with the attendant division of labor by biological sex. Crucially, within this shift, motherhood and all the domestic labor that comes with it—despite this being the literal *lifeblood* of the whole system—came to be positioned as the original "labor of love." This meant that no women could expect to get paid for the work she performed in the home, thus maximizing profits for the owning class by keeping down the cost of producing future tax-paying workers.

Meanwhile, a man's suitability for fatherhood came to be predicated on his social status and earning capacity, thus establishing the (sometimes equally oppressive) masculine sex-role of "provider." A role that is *not* underpinned by the same narrative that fatherhood is a man's natural, God-given role and one that he must selflessly dedicate himself to or forever be perceived as a failure and a traitor to the race. All of which supports the idea that whatever biological urge a woman may genuinely feel to procreate, it has at least been *enhanced* in order to maintain the gendered status quo.

This is something that sociologist Orna Donath explores further in her controversial *Regretting Motherhood*, in which she presents the findings of a study into mothers who openly admit to regretting having had kids. As with any subject this taboo, their testimony makes for edgy, compulsive reading. Central to these women's private agonies (one subject laments: "I am simply giving up my life. It is giving up too much, as far as I am concerned") are what Donath describes as the "feeling rules" of motherhood: the fact that only certain feelings about motherhood are allowed. This adds up to what she describes as "a colonization of the imagination."

You know what she's talking about, right? Feeling excited about becoming a mother: allowed. Dreading the loss of physical, mental, and emotional autonomy: definitely not. Feelings of elation any time a friend announces they are pregnant: lovely! Experiencing pangs of grief for the inevitable weakening of your bond, and feelings of jealousy toward the unborn child: *selfish fucking cunt*.

So, to what extent is the notion of the maternal instinct intertwined with these feeling rules? I'm not saying that anybody is "duped" into believing that they want kids. But any idea accompanied by strong emotional content tends to override logic. And what is more emotionally charged than the rose-tinted fantasy of motherly love? As Donath writes: "A woman might feel that she truly wants to become a mother, but this feeling is often awakened through the internalization of images and messages that depict motherhood as an exclusive means to what she actually desires—peace of mind, acceptance, wholeness." But in reality, the things that bring us peace of mind, acceptance, and a sense of wholeness are as diverse as we are. Meanwhile, as many of us have experienced as children ourselves, we know that parental love can equally be tinged with frustration, indifference, and even outright abuse.

Surely, at this point in our human story, any one individual's ability to override all of the above, and make a clear-eyed assessment of our actual suitability for parenthood, should be celebrated. After all, the option to decide whether we want to have kids, and who we want to have kids with, is a privilege that has been won by decades—if not centuries—of feminist resistance, and the fight for gender equality. A fight that suffered a severe setback with the overturning of *Roe v. Wade*. The extent to which women are still corralled into motherhood, as well as the inequities and the suffering that often result from this shows us how far there still is to go. As women without kids, I believe that our role is to continue to help level the playing field by confidently valorizing the path of non-motherhood, to help to change the narrative about who "should" become parents and why, and to shine a light on how to better to support people in this role. Within this context, our individual paths to non-motherhood become part of a movement toward greater autonomy and equality for all.

***

So how do we begin to shift the needle on the Mommy Binary, instead embracing the concept of the Motherhood Spectrum? First and foremost, we need to be able to speak openly and honestly about who we are as individuals and to share our deepest fears, needs, and desires for our lives. These are conversations we can begin to have with one another. It's often seen as "not polite" to inquire too deeply into a person's reasons for being a woman without kids. But this is yet more pronatalist conditioning, the implication being that a person not being a parent must be the result of a misfortune too tragic to mention. If anything, open, honest conversations about where we orient on the Motherhood Spectrum, and why, can be both validating and illuminating.

For example, around the time one of my best friends and I were both turning forty, as I was finding my confidence with my Affirmative No, she became entangled with what can seem to out-siders like the industrial birthing complex known as IVF. I walked the emotional tightrope with her, watching her go from hopeful and determined to disillusioned, tearful, and spent. Now that she's an ecstatic (if exhausted) mom to bouncing baby twins, I quizzed her about what had compelled her to keep going. I was hoping she'd be able to describe the baby fever that I had never been able to detect in myself—if it were biological, then surely it must be physical? In my imagination, this felt like a raging hunger, but in the heart space. But instead, she told me: "I loved big family holidays when I was a kid, and I wanted to re-create those experiences; I wanted a noisy house full of people because I was afraid of the opposite; I wanted to make my parents happy, and see them as grandparents."

Hearing her describe all this, I realized that her reasons *for* having kids were not unlike my reasons for *not*. Except where she craves noise, I need cleansing hours of silence in my days; and where she's excited for family trips to Disneyland, in my favorite childhood memories, I am by myself. As for seeing my parents as grandparents, I had a hard time picturing this (for reasons which will become clear). But there was also something else, which got closer to the mythical baby fever. When we spoke again a year or so later, she shared, "I felt like I had so much love to give that I would have done anything to have a child." And in my case, I realized I had always felt like this about my *ideas*. It was partly a compulsive need to say what I had to say about the world that had me apply the same dogged determination to my writing career.

Reflecting on this, it seems less like we are wired with a shared *biological imperative*. Rather, what we are fortunate enough to have in common is being born in an era when it is within our power to pursue the path we know is right for us. Even if a woman choosing a life of the mind over family life still means she will sometimes be perceived as heartless and uncaring.

But what about when you just *don't know* if motherhood is for you? It could be that you're reading this because you're like me; you never wanted kids, and you need to know you did not miss some great big memo in the sky. But perhaps you're still undecided, which in and of itself feels more like a no than a yes. If the opportunity passed you by, perhaps you have found yourself privately grieving your childlessness and unsure of what comes next. And if you're one of those moms who does not naturally revel in motherhood, perhaps you're looking for ways to explain to yourself why this is. Whatever the reason you're here, I believe that a full understanding of where we fall on the Motherhood Spectrum—and *why*—is key to understanding ourselves as part of an emerging and diverse *womankind*. Not to prove or to excuse anything, but to make our peace with diverging from a narrative that was written long before we got here. The better to untether our search for *meaning* and *fulfillment* from our capacity to procreate, and to engage with areas of life that have been ring-fenced by the conventions of motherhood—*purpose, family, love, legacy*—on our own terms.

When considering our place on the Motherhood Spectrum, let's look again to those elements that "make us who we are":

Temperament Your nature and how this affects your behavior; your role in group dynamics; your communication style; how you connect with others; your relationship to control; your need to fit in.

Circumstance Your lineage and family of origin; your cultural and social conditioning; your spiritual beliefs; your living situation and economic stability; your sexuality and gender expression; your career.

Fears What keeps you awake at night; the things you have an aversion to; situations and people you recoil from; what you feel the need to protect yourself from; what frightens you about the world.

Desires The things you want; what excites you and turns you on; the experiences you're drawn to; what you find pleasurable; how you like to spend your days; what you hope for your life and for the world.

Capacities What comes naturally to you; the things you have a talent for and are good at; what energizes you; what you bring to your relationships; the things others value about you.

Limitations What you are not good at; the things you find challenging and have little aptitude for; what drains you; what you are physically incapable of; the areas where you often make mistakes.

What comes up for you when feel deeply into these categories? Read through them again. Take your time with each and make lists. Write out the stories and memories that swim through your consciousness as you engage with this self-inquiry. Feel the feelings in your body that accompany these visions, and notice any other voices (your mom's? society's?) that want to make any of what you are noticing about yourself "right" or "wrong." I have included a specific list of questions to engage with at the end of this chapter to help guide you in this, but there is no correct way to feel about any of the above. A combination of nature and nurture, much of it is also beyond our control. There is only the person you are, the life you have lived, the influences you have been exposed to, and the degree of choice you have had access to along the way. Holding this position, ask yourself: *What stands out as my non-negotiables for living a worthwhile, contented, and meaningful life?*

The next step is to map what you have uncovered about your nature against what you also *know to be true* about motherhood. Not the Instagram version—but the raw, daily, down-in-the-trenches stuff of mothering that you have witnessed with your own eyes. What are your recollections of your personal experience of being mothered? What has been your mother's experience of mothering, and *her* mother's? How is it for your friends, your colleagues, and the members of your wider community? Do you see motherhood as a tender refuge from the competitive cut and thrust of the world outside the home? Or has a lack of financial and emotional support stretched the mothers in your life to a breaking point? Maybe it's a combination of both.

Given the emotional charge of the word "mother," now see what happens when you strip this away and instead place your non-negotiables within the context of *parenthood*. That is, the responsibility for feeding, sheltering, nurturing, and educating small human beings. The psychological, intellectual, moral, and emotional labor of raising well-rounded, secure adults. What version of yourself do you see in this picture? Is she largely content with her lot? Relishing being the mistress of her own universe and its subjects? Or is she harried, resentful, and out of her depth? Maybe, again, it's a combination of all of the above. Remember, there are no right or wrong answers, and none of what comes up makes you a good or a bad person.

Perhaps this exercise will help you feel more confident in your Affirmative No. Or if you always wanted kids and it hasn't happened for you, maybe it will inspire you to prioritize other ways to "mother" and to center children in your life. Remember, the change-making potential of our revolutionary sisterhood begins with each and every one of us owning, embracing, and sharing our diverse experiences of being women without kids.

Ultimately, there's no such thing as the "right" place to orient oneself on the Motherhood Spectrum—only the place that is right for you. There is also no one path to fulfillment, or any magic pill that will guarantee a happy life. In fact, in a short video on the subject of whether or not to have kids from The School of Life, a London-based philosophical organization, the narrator points out that every path we take inevitably leads to suffering. *Because in life, some degree of suffering is inevitable.* The key is to recognize which *kinds of suffering* you are best-suited and most resilient to, and, where possible, to adjust your trajectory accordingly. In terms of parenting, the video lists some of the suffering associated with having kids: disappointment with oneself as a parent, guilt, exhaustion, lost opportunities, and a messy house. Meanwhile, it wasn't any surprise to me that the "suffering" associated with *not* being a parent are not things that particularly bother me: lack of constant distraction/calls on one's time, society's message that one has "missed out," loneliness, boredom, and a sentimental longing for the comfort of children in old age. Being a confirmed introvert who tends to organize my days around how much alone time

I need, it also didn't surprise me to learn that extroverts tend to have more kids.[7]

This again goes against the notion that motherhood is the exclusive means to a woman's peace of mind, acceptance, and sense of wholeness. Ultimately, orienting toward a more meaningful life means investigating what the exalted, essential, non-negotiable YOU would be doing with your days if all the expectations and projections of family, friends, and the wider society were to fall away. The parts to focus on when considering this are your *desires and capacities*. What you *want* and what you are *good at*. What brings you *joy*. For so long, women have been told that our purpose, our contribution, and our joy will arrive by stork, swaddled in blankets and sucking its thumb. That if we fail, literally, to deliver, then we have essentially failed at life. But for anybody leaning toward the Affirmative No end of the Motherhood Spectrum, this will not necessarily be the case. Becoming a mom may only bring suffering that we are not so well-equipped to endure; it might be what finds us feeling like we've failed. And meanwhile, fulfillment may come in a different kind of package entirely.

***

For any woman without kids, the next step is to determine what, exactly, this might look like. As noted, following that trip to the therapist, I had instinctively spent the best part of my thirties weighing the personal pros and cons, the needs, wants, fears, and desires, that placed me at the Affirmative No end of the Motherhood Spectrum. But it was during this time that I also came as close as I have come to overriding my no. A few days after my thirty-eighth birthday, my fertility careering toward the edge of the proverbial cliff, S and I sat holding hands on a busy street in the pulsing humidity of a stormy night in Sydney, Australia.

The baby conversation had come up, and three glasses of wine to the wind, I squeezed his hand and asked: "We should just do it, shouldn't we?" We were ten thousand miles from our Brooklyn apartment, but wherever we went together felt like home. Why would we not want to expand the bubble of us? It's not like we hadn't discussed it before, but something about this time felt different. By the end of the night, we were agreed. Having a kid would be an adventure, an unbeatable once-in-a-lifetime experience! We would even call the child Sydney; the name worked for a girl or a boy. But when the booze buzz wore off, the feeling was the same as when I was planning a trip: anxious anticipation. Would I make all my connections okay?

But a baby is the literal opposite of a vacation, and our tipsy enthusiasm for the idea petered out like an engine sputtering to a stop. The following year I became an aunt, my adorable nephew a *spit*, the double in both *spirit and image*, of my lovely brother. My womb remained unmoved. And as everybody else became busily engaged with the daily onslaught of family life, any remaining curiosity or concern from others about my own ongoing nulliparous status began to recede like water draining from a river at low tide. *So that was that, then.* Quitting wondering when I would want to be a mom felt like both a big exhale and something of an anticlimax. A gradual stilling of choppy waters giving way to feelings of serenity, self-assurance, some sadness, and an open space of possibility stretched across my insides like a blank canvas.

Which meant that it was time to course correct, and to align myself more fully with whatever *was* my Affirmative Yes. And so it was also around age forty that I began to extricate my writing life from the glossy world of women's magazines that had been the bedrock of my career to date and I began living my own dream for my life as opposed to using my energetic output to sell an exploitative, airbrushed version of happiness and fulfillment on somebody else's behalf. Investigating what made life meaningful to me led me to launch an online platform dedicated to all things *numinous*, as I looked to the stars for answers and began to wonder what "spirituality" could mean for somebody raised atheist like me. In the years that followed, I would go on to publish my first book, get serious about quitting drinking, and begin to make peace with my personal demons once and for all.

I don't think it's a coincidence that many women without kids historically have been writers, therapists, and engaged in other ways with the creative and healing arts. Women who, beginning with their own process of self-reflection, have gone on to dedicate their lives to understanding and making peace with the more confusing psycho-emotional aspects of the human condition. Women who might also, in another era, have been given the label *witch*. Walking any path that diverges from the norm leads to the kind of internal self-inquiry that lends itself to vocations like these, which (whether undertaken professionally or not) tend to heal the self as surely as they heal others. I expect you can relate; a desire to better know yourself and your place in the world in which we live is likely why you're reading this.

Not that many mothers are not also engaged in this kind of work. But with no child to dedicate one's nurturing energies to, women without kids are by default buying themselves more time and space for their own personal development—time and space that is a rare enough commodity already in a capitalist society that demands constant productivity. It's interesting that this is also often framed as "naval-gazing," as if a woman who makes her healing and her personal growth the focus of her life is somehow searching for the missing umbilical cord. When in fact, if "hurt people hurt people"—endlessly projecting our unprocessed pain onto others and thus creating more suffering in the world—then healing our own shit before handing it down for the next generation to fix is as valid a contribution to society as any. A "purpose" in and of itself.

This is a concept we will revisit throughout this text. It forms the basis of my further-reaching theories about what it really means to be a woman without kids and the truly revolutionary nature of this orientation. Within this, we will see that in decoupling our destinies from a very old story about women's rightful role in society, something is ending with us. That rather than a loss, this is how we begin to imagine a legacy for womankind beyond motherhood.

* * *

Use the following questions to help you orient yourself on the Motherhood Spectrum. When answering, map your responses against how you imagine your life as a parent. Start with a few questions, and take your time with them so as not to overwhelm yourself. Gradually come back and answer more as you feel ready. Revisit this self-inquiry often, trust whatever arises, and notice how your responses change over time (perhaps during the course of reading this book). Remember, there is no right or wrong, only what is true for you.

1. What are the first words that you associate with "mother"?

2. What style of mothering did you experience yourself?

3. What did you enjoy most and least about being a child?

4. What did you want most for yourself when you envisioned your life as an adult?

5. How important is family to you?

6. Who were your first role models—and who inspires you now?

7. What are your unique gifts, and how have you been able to utilize them in your life?

8. What untapped potential is still inside you?

9. What kinds of activities do you enjoy the most?

10. What kinds of activities do you find the most challenging?

11. What makes you lose your temper?

12. When do you feel the most content?

13. What, if anything, is missing from your life?

14. How do you feel about spending time on your own?

15. What role does sex play in your life?

16. Which of your achievements are you proudest of?

17. What do you fear most about the future?

18. How are you preparing yourself—materially and emotionally—for growing older?

19. What does the concept of "legacy" mean to you?

20. How do you picture the final years of your life?

"

"I vividly remember being a toddler and one day thinking to myself, 'Yeah no, I don't ever want kids.' I cannot tell you why or where that came from, and I've never wavered since."

**— age forty-seven,
in a common-law relationship**

"I never saw my parents hug, kiss, or show affection or love towards one another. They were never mean to each other, but that almost made it worse. Both sets of grandparents were the same. I never thought of their lack of love towards one another as impacting my desire not to have children, but I know I wouldn't want children growing up in that kind of environment."

— age thirty, in a new relationship

"My mother had a rocky relationship with her mother, which influenced her greatly, of course. I am so scared that this is part of my karmic path or destiny. I don't want to repeat that history. On the other hand, I find that my awareness of it is already changing the pattern."

— age thirty-one, married

"

CHAPTER 2

Origin Stories

MY BROTHER'S HOME BIRTH when I was three-and-a-half years old is my first full-color memory; it was the day I became fully conscious of myself both as an individual and as part of my family of origin. Mum and I had been preparing for the event, which would take place in our tiny two-up, two-down cottage in the sleepy riverside village in Suffolk where I grew up, for weeks. It was 1979. A home birth, all natural, fit with the earthy ethos of mum and her friends, who also baked their own buckwheat bread, sewed their own clothes, and took classes in shiatsu massage. I'd helped pick out the comfy wicker chair with the black chevron design in the weave for the midwife at the big department store; had watched mum's belly and breasts swell, day by day, as she appeared to shrink in comparison. As the due date drew closer, she grew softer and squishier, firm toffee turning to soft marshmallow. As for the birth itself, I had no idea what to expect. But given the air of excited anticipation that had permeated our simple, DIY existence, it was evident that something *major* was about to go down.

The event itself was equal parts magical and terrifying. In my memory, there was a terrible storm that night, our little home coming alive with an electric, supernatural force. Meanwhile, my brother's arrival sucked up mum's attention like a hungry vacuum. As an infant, he cried all the time and rarely slept; once he could walk and talk, our little cottage was a nonstop chaos of commotion and clutter. It felt like there was never enough of her for both of us, and his needs being so much louder, he got the lion's share. Dad lived in London and was only around on weekends, and this found me by myself a lot of the time; I would spend hours drawing and reading, dreaming dreams of adventures in faraway lands, and learning the names of the flowers that studded the hedgerows lining the local village lanes. Given that both my parents were somewhat estranged from their families, there was also never a sense of our hand-stitched little unit being part of a larger, interconnected web of care. There were no grandparents on hand to hold the baby and give my mother a break, while visits with aunts, uncles, and cousins felt like a duty to be endured, like eating our greens.

But still, these were my people. From my mother, I inherited an entrepreneurial work ethic and an intense sensitivity to my environment; from my father, his wavy blonde hair, blue-gray eyes, and intellectual curiosity about life. But it would take another four decades for me to fully unpack the *emotional inheritance* my parents handed down to me; that is, the feeling tone that has colored my existence, and the default emotional responses to life that they in turn had been imprinted with by our shared ancestry. In her book on the subject, psychologist Galit Atlas explains that this emotional inheritance—which is passed from parent to child, down the generations in our DNA—is often tangled up in the "silenced experiences that belong not only to us but to our parents, grandparents, and great-grandparents." The unspeakable traumas and family secrets, she means, which, when left to fester, "often keep us from living to our full potential. They affect our mental and physical health, create gaps between what we want for ourselves and what we are able to have, and haunt us like ghosts."

So why am I telling you all this? In the previous chapter, I suggested that something is *ending with us* when for whatever reason we do not procreate. Now, I want us to dig deeper into what this might mean on an individual level.

In my case, I would grow up to discover that I had been cosmically assigned to a family system marked by disinterest, disapproval, and distance. Unlike my friend with the twins in the previous chapter, my experience of "family" is not something I have felt called to replicate—in fact, by the age of five I had already informed my mother that I would not be having any children of my own. "If do I ever have a baby, I'll give it to you to look after," she remembers me telling her. But then my brother would go on to embrace fatherhood like he was born for the role, and there is also little official data to link childlessness or maternal ambivalence with family dysfunction. After all, most people become parents—while the most recent statistics show that 70–80 percent of individuals describe their family as being "dysfunctional."[8] This suggests that the majority of people who grew up in less than idyllic homes go on to have kids of their own, many with the express purpose of righting wrongs and doing things differently. Likewise, there are those who emerge from their childhoods seemingly unscathed and who choose not to procreate.

But whatever the case, given the extent to which our early influences shape who we become as adults, there are sure to be elements of your own upbringing that help to explain how you feel about motherhood today—and which will help you to orient yourself on the Motherhood Spectrum. The women in my survey cited everything from growing up in an unhappy home, to having had a completely selfless mother as being factors in their own decisions not to have kids. What scenes from your childhood are playing as you read this? What was the feeling tone of your childhood home, and how would you feel about potentially reliving this as a mother yourself? How might your emotional inheritance have colored your feelings about becoming a parent?

Any one person's reproductive outcomes are rarely as clear-cut as us simply replicating or rejecting what we experienced as children ourselves, but one thing is for certain: not having kids means a chapter in our ancestry is closing. This realization can be freeing, and it can feel like a loss in and of itself. As if the stream of *life* that has flowed from mother to mother, animating all those who came before us, is stuttering to a sad, lonely stop. But what if, as well as an ending, we saw this as a new beginning? A diversion onto a life-path that might leave a different kind of legacy? What if being a woman without kids was less about lopping off branches that have become diseased, and more a pruning of the family tree, the better to encourage new growth?

* * *

In a way, embracing our lives and our legacies as women without kids must begin with an acknowledgment of our families of origin—and specifically the ways in which the experiences of our mothers, and their mothers before them, have shaped us. These are the individuals that literally made us who we are today, and it is part of our evolutionary path to simultaneously emulate and reject their influence, taking what works and leaving behind what doesn't. This is how evolution works; as such, we are both destined to follow in their footsteps and to seek to improve on their lot.

Given what we've learned about the toxic origins of patriarchal motherhood and the unequal power dynamics and abuses of power therein, the truth is that many of our mothers, and their mothers, and their mothers' mothers before them suffered unnecessarily in their mothering. Is it any wonder that more and more of us, now that we have the choice, are questioning whether parenthood is for us? In some ways, forgoing motherhood is the ultimate course correction.

Meanwhile, families become "dysfunctional" when the behavior patterns and coping mechanisms that have been passed down the generations like dusty heirlooms no longer serve the material well-being and the healthy emotional expression of the individuals making up the family system.

For example, our foremothers' literal dependence on men for their material security may have led to unhealthy patterns of codependency in our relationships. Elsewhere, it may have felt at one point like it was in the best interests of our ancestors to deny or override any leanings toward homosexuality—an emotional inheritance that might have manifested in future generations as homophobia or shame about being queer. When we map this concept against the rising numbers of women without kids, you could say we are staging a mass intervention of sorts: a handing-back of a *collective* emotional inheritance—the emotional inheritance of patriarchy—that no longer serves us. Something that was simply not available to the women who preceded us.

The term "dysfunctional family" first appeared in print in 1974, in Salvador Minuchin's *Families and Family Therapy*. This suggests that it is only in the past five decades—corresponding with advances in women's and queer rights, along with the steady drop-off in the birth rate—that much familial dysfunction has even come to be seen as such. A shocking illustration of this is the fact that marital rape was legal in the United States until 1975 and was only outlawed in all fifty states as late as 1993.[9] The emotional inheritance of *this*? The belief that men are entitled to the owner-ship of women's bodies. Physical and sexual abuse being more extreme examples of family dysfunction, with denial, the keep-ing of secrets, a lack of clear boundaries, substance abuse, anger issues, conflict among family members, and favoritism all being hallmarks of dysfunctional home environments.

But let's get real here for a minute: if up to 80 percent of people consider their families to be dysfunctional, then isn't it the case that this is actually *just how families have come to function under centuries of patriarchy?* The layers of oppression, inequity, and resentment calcifying over time, until somebody takes on the task of tackling the buildup. And if this is the case, then questioning whether motherhood is for us—that is, *questioning whether we want to reproduce more of the same*—suggests a level of awareness, perhaps unconscious, that there is something to be looked at in this area before we go ahead and procreate.

After all, it is far harder to override the conditioning of our origin stories once we become parents ourselves, since we are pre-destined to pass on the emotional inheritance that *we* received without us even noticing. This process begins at the moment of conception, with subtle chemical signals about our mother's mental and emotional state being absorbed with the nutrients from her food in utero.[10] Now, the only way to stop the patterns repeating in our kids is to consistently override the default beliefs and coping mechanisms of our lineage. This process can be as painful, as ardu-ous, and as expensive (if undertaken with the help of a therapist, for example) as to prevent the vast majority of people from engaging with it. Especially parents, for whom time, energy, and financial resources are often already stretched to the limit.

But *disrupting the default beliefs and coping mechanisms of our lin-eage* is essential work for anybody who wants to create a life that feels meaningful to them—a life where we know who we really are and where we feel confident about expressing this "full" self and bringing it to our relationships with others. A life where we don't find our-selves endlessly reliving the same old shit and stuck in the same old "stuff" about money, love, and self-worth. Ending up at the same frustrating emotional dead ends. Consuming endless crap, numbing with endless substances, and embroiling ourselves in endless dramas to distract from the fact that we feel like *we're living somebody else's life*—a life, perhaps, where it's like we are continuing to suffer on our ancestors' behalf.

All of which is pretty complex stuff, so let's pause here and take a moment to reflect. Consider: what are the specifics of the emotional inheritance that was handed down to you by your parents, and their parents before them? Meaning, what are your default reactions to challenging situations, and in what ways do these coping mechanisms tend to hold you back? Now picture yourself being confronted with the challenges of parenthood—the lack of sleep and privacy, the unpredictable nature of any external influences on the family unit, and the financial pressure of having additional bodies to house and mouths to feed. What parts of your emotional inheritance might be triggered in these situations—and what would it take for you to override these triggers and do things differently?

It quickly becomes easy to see how, on a purely practical level, it is simply easier to engage with the work of intergenerational pattern-breaking when you don't have kids. Although this is something that more and more "conscious parents" are engaging with—my own mother included.

The pervasive atmosphere of my early childhood was one of constant mending and tending to, life unfolding in a perpetual series of small catastrophes that required endless tinctures, talismans, and trips to the osteopath. By the time I was twelve, there was a copy of *I'm OK—You're OK* on my mother's nightstand, and her commitment to her *self-healing* found her attending conscious parenting groups. "We don't use labels," she'd remind us. "I am not angry. I *feel* angry about what just happened." Eventually, she trained to become a psychotherapist herself. The first person in her family to engage with this kind of self-work, this became a new thread in the emotional inheritance she handed down to me. For her, her self-healing had centered on breaking the patterns of *her* origin story; in some ways, this helped clear the way for me to confidently write a whole new story.

But while both my parents were committed to doing things differently than their parents before them, still they couldn't help imprinting me with the feelings of estrangement and alienation that have permeated our shared lineage—and which have also influenced my decision not to become a parent myself. I will share some more details from my origin story here to show you what I mean. Remember: uniting our unsung sisterhood begins with us sharing our stories with one another, the better to understand *and accept* the diversity of influences that have made us women without kids.

After I began to look seriously at why I'd never wanted to be a mom, I went through a phase of wondering how my parents had even managed to have me. They were just so *different*. Picturing them as a couple—let alone as *co-parents*—was like walking around in a pair of mismatched shoes. My dad so tall, fair, and philosophically minded; my mum a full foot shorter, with curly black hair, and big, volatile feelings that were always simmering close to the surface. Like over 50 percent of pregnancies in the United Kingdom and the United States, my arrival was unplanned—and while my mother wanted nothing more than to be a traditional, stay-at-home mum, Dad claims he'd never intended to have children. In her case, having been shipped off to boarding school at age eleven and losing her mother to uterine cancer when she was eighteen meant she yearned to create the loving family for herself that she felt she had never had. Taking into account the mismatch in my parents' personalities and expectations for their union, it is not surprising to me that their unconventional marriage did not last—despite their best efforts to accommodate each other's needs.

If they had one thing in common, shared with so many kids of their boomer generation, it was a misogynistic and largely absent patriarch, and a mother who had borne the brunt of this. My grandfathers' unthinking cruelty, their mistreatment of their wives, and their indifference toward their children were legendary in our household; but back then, this kind of behavior was not only excused, it was often expected. "My father lives on a different planet," my mother would declare angrily after another failed attempt to connect with her distant and dictatorial RAF "Wing Commander" father, her dark eyes brimming with hurt. He'd remarried within months of her mother passing, and his new wife made it clear she had no interest in providing a home for my mother and her siblings.

Meanwhile, "Sir Peter," my paternal grandpa, was super-charismatic, granted a hall pass for his many infidelities by his celebrated self-made success; he'd received a knighthood from none other than Queen Elizabeth herself for services to the field of architecture following World War II. When we visited, he would make origami mice out of paper napkins to amuse my brother and I, referring to me only as "girl," while my grandmother sat humming to herself at the top of the table, heavily medicated on "mother's little helpers" (Valium) and occasionally blowing the air out of her mouth with a little "prrrrf."

My dad's parents' house was in a fancy part of town, but it felt cold and uninviting and always smelled of cat piss. As with our other relatives, visits were kept to a minimum, each point of contact a physical reminder of the feeling tone of our family system: suppression, faking it, hurt feelings, and secrets nursed like open sores. Dad's sister, Sarah, had disowned the family and done a disappearing act at age eighteen, when she emigrated to America. All of which, combined, meant that by the time my brother was born, it really did feel like it was *just us*.

Not that anything about my origin story is particularly unusual or traumatic—especially given what we've learned about the prevalence of family dysfunction. And still, I always knew I didn't want "a family" (i.e., kids) of my own. Growing up, I also remember wondering why people were so obsessed with babies. I didn't get it; infant humans were ugly, wrinkled, overgrown worms, their thrusting little bodies as fragile as glass.

Do not drop! Eyes encrusted with gunk, gummy pink mouths leaking drool. The dreadful wailing. The constant aura of poop. And the *power* they wielded. When there was a baby in the room everything revolved around them, the atoms of the air itself rearranging themselves to funnel all attention in the direction of the squawking, terrifying infant.

Was I secretly resentful of my baby brother's arrival on the scene? Or had I perhaps inherited my father's attitude to parenthood along with his physical attributes? Possibly a bit of both. According to a book from The School of Life titled *How to Overcome Your Childhood*, something else was going on, too.

To this day, being around infants and very young children can bring up intense feelings of discomfort in me. I am completely intimidated by their volatile neediness, as if one wrong move on my part might either do irreparable damage or trigger an epic meltdown. In the book, the authors claim that such a "dislike" of babies stems from them being so utterly *useless*—so messy, so vulnerable, and so incompetent—that their very existence reflects back to us the same messy, vulnerable incompetence that we cannot bear to accept in ourselves. Messy, vulnerable incompetence that is often part and parcel of becoming a mom. But how had I learned to disavow these "babyish" parts of myself so young?

In her beautiful memoir, *Good Morning, Destroyer of Men's Souls*, which doubles as a study of codependency, Nina Renata Aron writes about "a tendency, particularly common in daughters among 'dysfunctional' families, to overcompensate for parental inadequacies by becoming parentified and developing an excessive sensitivity to the needs of others." Reading these lines, I immediately flashed on Mum, strung-out and often tearful as she struggled as a de facto single parent. In my role as eldest child and big sister, I became a sponge for her anxieties about the lack of funds in the bank, her fraught relations with her relatives, her fears about my brother's health. Adding to her stressors, he'd contracted bacterial meningitis at ten months old and spent two weeks in intensive care; when Dad took me to the hospital to visit, my brother had life-saving antibiotics being pumped directly into the lining of his infant brain through a fragile tower made of plaster of paris.

Whatever needs I might have had seemed inconvenient and insignificant by comparison; when my mother hugged me, it always felt like it was because *she* wanted comfort. Comfort that, as a child, I was not equipped to give her—and that, in turn, I learned not to need from her. Perhaps you can relate: among the women in my survey, a significant number expressed feeling responsible on some level for their mothers, whether emotionally, financially, or both. "[My mother] has suffered mentally my whole life, and I have parented her and my three siblings. My fear is that I will turn into her if I have kids," one woman wrote.

A bookish kid like me, Aron also shares that her love of reading stemmed from the fact that "I just wanted cozy quiet: a fantasy of detachment from the webs of accountability in which I already felt puzzlingly ensnared." Cut to eight-, nine-, ten-year-old me, curled into the corner of our pink velour sofa, our calico cat Delilah on my lap, the ideal self of my imagination five thousand miles away, dancing down the halls of *Sweet Valley High*. Topping up my tan in the California sun with troublemaker Jessica; wishing I didn't identify so much more strongly with goodie-two-shoes Elizabeth. Only faintly aware of Mum's frenetic juggling of her work with her domestic chores; pushing down my guilt at not offering to help her out more often. "You have no compassion!" she once yelled at me when I complained about her asking me to do the dishes, the dirty pans and unpaid bills towering over us like the gnarled branches of our family tree.

What I internalized was: "You have no idea how hard it is to be me." This may well ring true for you, too, given the challenges of parenting in a society that provides little in the way of real support for mothers and their kids. Digging deeper here, what do you know about the kinds of suffering that the mothers in your lineage experienced as the result of a lack of proper emotional or financial support? How did this impact your experience of being mothered—and perhaps your feelings about becoming a mother yourself?

In my case, with this whole domestic setup, this precarious balancing act of an existence, this constant shapeshifting to accommodate other people's feelings and needs—on a subconscious level I had evidently decided early on that it was not for me. Like my parents before me, detaching from my family of origin and carving my own path seemed like it would also be my destiny.

* * *

As fate would have it, I followed in my Aunt Sarah's footsteps and moved to America when S got a job in New York. I was thirty-five at the time—the age when most of the women in my life were beginning to get serious about having kids. Turns out this also made me the third generation of sisters on my dad's side of the family to start afresh and put down *new roots* in the United States. My Great Aunt Ursula, whose existence I only learned of recently, had started the trend, moving to Washington, DC, to take a job at the World Bank. Another woman without kids, she also remained unmarried: "She was a lesbian," my dad told me when I asked about her. Apparently, she had been expunged from the family history due to speculation about her sexuality.

When I arrived stateside, it was 2012 and the emerging "now age" wellness scene of New York City, a melting pot of crystals, green juice, and self-anointed gurus, was the perfect setting in which to begin to unpack the issues that had followed me across the Atlantic like a soggy rain cloud (*drinking too much; the constant pressure I put on myself; the feeling that nothing I did, or achieved, or earned would ever be enough*). I had already been formulating plans for my numinous lifestyle blog, and in the name of research I laid myself down at the feet of shamans, energy workers, and astrologers, offered up my palms to be read, imbibed elixirs infused with magical dust, and sobbed the emotional gunk out of my cells in breathwork circles that left me feeling spent and eerily at peace. All of it promised a deeper connection to my *authentic self.* Cut adrift from my family of origin and three thousand miles from home, I found myself asking: *Who was the "self" I'd been posing as for the first half of my life?*

It was during this period that I discovered a form of group therapy called "Family Constellations," which involves the study of our family stories and how to heal from them. As such, the practice can also provide profound insights into what it means to be a woman without kids. The theory goes that we each have a natural "place" within our family system, and that when a past family member couldn't take his or her place—due perhaps to sickness, war, abandonment, divorce, or family estrangement—a member of the next generation is recruited to take that place instead, in an attempt to "fix" the system. In addition, any unresolved traumas experienced by members of the previous generation will be repeated as they attempt to seek a better outcome. But until we consciously choose to disrupt it—one way to do this being *not to procreate*—all that happens is a perpetuation of the trauma and/or dysfunction.

In the energetically charged environment of a session, the facilitator Marine Sélénée assured me, I would have the opportunity to hand whatever baggage I'd been carrying on behalf of earlier family members back to whomever it belonged. In doing so, not only would I free myself, but the ripple effect would be felt going back generations, like a cosmic chiropractor traveling back in time to pop the bones of the past back into place.

When I showed up at Marine's apartment in SoHo, I was ushered into a circle with two other women who seemed as nervous as me. I never discovered their names; unlike with traditional therapy, there is very little talking. Instead, over the course of the following two hours, we would each stand in for the various players in each other's family dramas, physical placeholders for the energetic imprints of the missing persons. When my turn came, it was like time and space fell away, as the edges of my vision blurred to nothingness. Marine invited my "mother" to turn and face me. In that moment, I saw myself *as my mother's mother*, the grandmother I had never known, while the face of the woman in front of me morphed into that of my mum as a little girl: *my child*. A wave of emotion churned the sediment at the bottom of my being, and I was wracked with sobs: in that moment, it was like I was embodying three generations of women grappling with a loss, the death of my grandmother, that had never been grieved. The experience was psychedelic, like therapy on acid.

Marine describes her work as a process of "taking care of what was so we can be fully with what is." But on a felt as opposed to an intellectual level. In my case, that first session was the beginning of a years-long process of healing my connection to my mother and the maternal grandmother I had never known. Given what the practice tells us about future generations being recruited to resolve the traumas of the past, the strange "coincidence" of both myself and my Aunt Sarah having followed in Ursula's footsteps by relocating to the United States also takes on a profound significance. To what extent was our mutual defection connected to Ursula's estrangement from our family system? Reflecting on this, is there anybody in your family system that you feel cosmically connected to in this way? In Marine's book, *Connected Fates, Separate Destinies*, she suggests creating an alter for any ancestors you want to honor with your life—as a way to begin healing any ruptures in your origin story.

When I asked Marine what it means from a Family Constellations perspective to be a woman without kids, she told it to me straight: "Most of the time this means the family system has suffered too much to carry a new generation, as there has been too much trauma, abuse, and neglect." Specifically, it may also indicate that there have been issues with oppression of the feminine principal and sexual abuse—*perhaps not in our lifetime, and unbeknownst to us*. If a fear of childbirth is contributing to any reluctance about having kids, it could be that an ancestor died while giving birth. In some cases, "If she is the only child, or if none of her siblings have kids, it also means the end of the family system." Does any of this ring true for you?

The family having *suffered too much to carry a new generation*. Sounds kind of extreme, right? But what if it also means that something is on its way to being resolved? That there is no need for the suffering of previous generations to keep being replicated in another attempt for it to be healed? The abortion that I'd had at age twenty-three had also come up in the work we did together; Marine insisted it was vital to include any and all "children" in our sessions, since all unborn souls are still part of the family system. Even I'd been shocked at the time by how easy it had been for me to decide to end my pregnancy. But what if part of me believed that I was in fact saving my unborn child from becoming embroiled in yet another cycle of the same old family dysfunction?

After all, working with Marine had helped bring to consciousness something else that I had intuited all along: that not becoming a mother myself would mean putting a stop to the unnecessary suffering of the mothers in my lineage. In the years since, I have uncovered yet more stories of estrangement and abuse among the women on both sides of my family tree, often manifesting in outcomes of abandonment, mental illness, and destitution. My not having kids, and my putting my life and my needs first while working to create financial security for myself, would mean turning my back on this emotional inheritance; an emotional inheritance that was at the heart of all the issues I had taken to that Spitalfields therapist.

Now let's layer this idea over the current mass rejection of patriarchal motherhood—a fundamental factor in women's historical dependence on men and in our foremothers' overall lack of say in how their lives played out. All of this is part of our *collective* emotional inheritance as women and woman-identifying individuals. When we look at it this way, the revolutionary rise of women without kids carries a clear message: collectively, we are ready to put a stop to the suffering experienced by women, mothers, and children under patriarchy.

Aren't we? The sheer scale with which twenty-first-century women are foregoing motherhood—whatever our reasons for this—or else rewriting the rules of parenting entirely, suggests that the casual, everyday suffering wrought on families, and mothers in particular, by centuries of gender inequality has reached a point where it can no longer be tolerated, can no longer be explained away as *just the way things are*. I believe we have reached a point in our consciousness raising, thanks to over a century of psychoanalysis, the ongoing fight for civil rights, and three generations' worth of self-help, where we are ready to take on the work of healing our personal and collective origin stories. After all, topics currently trending among self-help gurus and social media psychologists alike—from the concept of "reparenting" to codependency and attachment theory—point to an explosion of awareness about the impact of intergenerational trauma and a yearning to understand our collective emotional wounding in this area. Together they suggest a burning desire to disrupt ways of doing and being that have caused so much suffering to people and planet. To do things differently in our own lifetimes.

For women without kids, the invitation is to engage in this work *without getting another generation involved*. Think about it: what would it have meant for the women in your lineage not to have had kids? What sacrifices might they have had to make in order to pursue an alternative path? And how might their lives have played out differently had they been free to opt out of patriarchal motherhood? Could it be that more women having fewer kids today is paving the way for future generations to continue to enact these freedoms on their behalf?

As for how this will play out in any one individual's life, this will be unique to them based on the specifics of their lineage, the gifts they were born with, the structural issues impacting their choices, and the avenues for change that they have access to. But it will always begin with an honest and fearless investigation into how the experiences of those who came before us have helped shape who we are today. It will mean reckoning with the suffering they encountered in their lifetimes, and noticing where our default emotional responses to life mean we are continuing to suffer on their behalf—as opposed to boldly saying *no* to all of that and walking our own path.

This in turn will mean learning to differentiate between the *unconscious suffering* that keeps us stuck, reliving the patterns of the past, and the *conscious suffering*, the suffering of growth, that is beckoning us toward a more expansive fate. The conscious suffering, that is, of going against familial and societal expectations, and that can even be part of what creates a more meaningful life. For many women without kids, this will also mean living every day in defiance of the conditioning that says a woman is only as valuable as her reproductive capacity—as we continue to be confronted with this message time and again, in subtle and not-so-subtle ways.

When we really feel into what is ending with us when we divest from the more painful and limiting aspects of our origin stories, we can feel resentful of the hand we've been dealt—and righteously so in cases of more severe family trauma and abuse. But the only way to thrive as authentic, autonomous individuals, *so as not to perpetuate more of the same*, is to accept and live the life that we've been given, while taking whatever actions are in our power to do right by our ancestry and reconcile the reality of our lives today with the inheritance of our past. For women without kids, no matter how we got here, the path is clear for us to live unapologetically as the people we were born to be, and in doing so to boldly blaze a trail for generations of women to come.

"

"As an Arab-American, you are not considered a woman unless you are a mother. So I will always be viewed as a simple-minded girl, or as a spinster."

— **age thirty-five, single**

"I do not want any part in having my own children. There's something inside of my female body that completely rejects the notion of having children just because it can and because society makes us feel like it is the only thing we're good for."

— **age thirty, in a new relationship**

"I identify as queer and for many years felt that I was a man trapped inside a woman's body. I have recognized, though, that it was because of cultural conditioning that I felt 'other' than what a woman is supposed to be. I have now fully embraced the divine feminine aspect of myself and love that I am a more masculine woman."

— **age thirty-four, twice divorced**

"

CHAPTER 3

If Not Mother

AFTER MY PARENTS' DIVORCE was final, Mum moved us to London so that we could be closer to Dad. She wanted to make it easier for us to see him, she explained. It was 1985. In London, all the buildings were big, and the streets were filled with people you never saw more than once. Swapping sleepy country lanes for the sophistication of the city felt like one step closer to being a grownup—and at age nine, I could not wait to be a full-grown *woman*. This was also the year that the Madonna classic *Desperately Seeking Susan* came out—a move and a movie that would make for an intoxicating cocktail of influence when it came to my ideas about what this even meant.

Given that I was too young to see the movie in a theater, and taking into account that it would have taken a year or so for it to be released on VHS back then, let's assume that I was ten years old when I sunk into Dad's battered corduroy sofa with the cat-scratched arms, squished between my brother and Dad's new girlfriend, to watch the film. I snuck a sideways glance at her. She was ten years younger than my father and as tall as him. She had a loud, confident laugh, and she wore her hair in a sleek, shiny bob. I got the feeling she was also part of the reason we'd moved to the city.

Madonna's character in the film, the Susan of the title, was a gum-chewing, loose-limbed rock chick who lived out of a battered drum case lined with pink satin and adorned with graffiti skulls. I couldn't take my eyes off her. Watching the scene where she arrived in New York City at the Port Authority Bus Terminal, headed to the restroom, blasted her underarms with the hand drier, and opened up the case to change into a black lace tank, it was as if I had been picked up from my spot on the sofa and transported into my future.

The following Saturday, Dad's girlfriend took me on a shopping trip to North London's Camden Market to look for a bag like Susan's. The suitcase was its own character in the movie, spilling over with stolen jewelry, club fliers, ripped T-shirts, and vintage lingerie. Never had I needed something in my life so badly. And so we found ourselves, the girlfriend and I, pushing through the Camden crush of tourists, club kids, and aging punks, the oniony scent of Malaysian fried noodles hanging in the air like an exotic, savory curtain. We spent hours scouring the sprawling mini city of market stalls, but nothing quite conjured the same aura of *feminine anarchy* as the case in the movie. The closest we could find was a patent leather hatbox with a chunky silver clasp and a faux-fur leopard-print lid. Back home, I filled it with my sketchbooks; at night, the bedtime stories I told myself beneath the velvet blanket of the dark played to the soundtrack of "Get into the Groove."

I used to draw pictures of birds and hedgerow flowers; now, I spent hours sketching models wearing *outfits*, the price of each item listed carefully like I'd seen in the glossy magazines. When I got out of the bath, I would wrap the towel around my chest, willing my narrow body to hurry up and grow breasts. Getting ready for school, I pictured myself working in an office one day, like the one in *Thirtysomething*, the show we watched with Dad and his girlfriend on weekends. When I was a grownup, I would be able to earn my own money, choose all my own clothes, and live wherever I wanted.

But nowhere in my future as a woman did I see myself as a mom. Having grown up around pregnant and nursing women, it was clear to me that women and babies went together like hot milk and honey. As for my mum, she worked because she had to; her primary and most precious identity was that of "mother." But as I matured, and the potential paths my life might take began to reveal themselves, the womanly experiences of pregnancy, childbirth, and childrearing did not even cross my mind as possibilities to be rejected. Which just wasn't normal. *Was it?* Girl children are indoctrinated with the message that womanhood is synonymous with motherhood from the word *go. Aren't we?*

Until relatively recently, the answer to the above has been an unequivocal yes. Being female has meant being socialized to aspire to the role of mother. But the pervasive ambivalence about motherhood among my generation and younger, and the numbers in which we are either putting it off or opting out full stop, suggests that this is no longer the case—*that we are the ones who are destined to rewrite this script for good.* After all, the past four decades have also brought forth untold alternative role models for what a woman can be—and more emerge with each new generation. She is an artist, a director, a CEO. A traveler, an activist, a whistleblower, a W.I.T.C.H. (Woman in Total Control of Herself). She is the vice president of the United States. She is trans; she can even be a he or a they.

The question *What is woman if not mother?* used to draw a blank at best. But I say she is whoever the fuck she wants to be. In some ways, forgoing motherhood in favor of doing *literally anything else with your life* is the final frontier in women's fight for equality. The ultimate expression of *my body, my choice.* So why is it, then, that outside of a few progressive circles, non-motherhood remains such a stigmatized, deviant path? Why, no matter what other roles she might perform and what other roads she may travel down in her life, is a woman *still* not seen as complete until she becomes a mom? I believe the game-changing potential of our unsung sisterhood lies in the answers to these questions—so let's dive in.

When I began working on this manuscript, I was coming to the subject matter from the position of "outsider." As established, as somebody who never wanted kids, I had always felt different. *Othered*. I wanted to write a book that would speak to others in my position, as well as to any woman who has ever questioned whether motherhood was for her or who has tried and "failed" to become a mom. My primary intention here is to help my readers feel less like the freaks of nature that we are often painted as. As also noted, I have come to believe that *the majority* of women coming of age at the turn of the new millennium are destined to experience some degree of ambivalence about being a mom. To fall somewhere short of the Affirmative Yes end of the Motherhood Spectrum.

But while I had grown up feeling like "the only one," by the time I reached my early forties, something interesting began to happen: I was meeting more and more women my age and younger who were either actively pursuing an alternative legacy or for whom motherhood just hadn't happened. This had something to do with me having followed in Madonna's Susan character's footsteps and moved to New York City, a town that tends to attract women with bigger-than-average ambitions for our lives. But as other women without kids began to emerge in my life like rocks in the sand at low tide, I found myself asking: *had they been there all along?* Quietly weighing the pros and cons, anxiously heeding the ticking of their biological clocks, while making other choices that had led to other things?

It also dawned on me that the year I was born, 1976, sat slap bang in the middle of the decade when the tide had really begun to turn. That what I was in fact witnessing was the *natural outcome* of a half-century that had finally given women access to effective birth control and legal abortion, along with the means to seek financial independence. Like, once women actually *had the option* to pursue alternative paths to those of wife and mother, it seemed only logical that we'd have fewer kids, and that some of us would have none at all. That we might have seen a steeper drop-off in the birthrate far sooner had these developments come along earlier. It also makes sense that the extent to which this would impact the birthrate overall would not be immediately obvious until the *daughters* of the women's liberation movement—that is, any woman born from the mid-1960s onward—had reached the end of our childbearing years. That is, round about *now*.

Following the introduction of oral birth control in the early 1960s, abortion was legalized in 1968 and 1973 in the United Kingdom and United States, respectively. Meanwhile, the 1970s were also the backdrop to a messy, protracted (and ongoing) fight for the ratification of the Equal Rights Amendment (ERA) in the United States, a bill designed to guarantee equal legal rights in matters of divorce, property, and employment for all American citizens, regardless of sex. The ERA was seen as integral to gender equality *not least* because it would help to decouple a woman's value to society from her role as mother. As we've seen, until this point, many women had been largely dependent on men for their financial security. In exchange for this, they were expected to "earn their keep" in the role of homemaker, their contribution to the economy being the production of the future labor force.

By enabling women to seek financial independence, the ERA would, in theory, free women to pursue whatever life paths they wanted, as well as to escape situations where an unequal power (read: financial) dynamic had left them subject to domestic abuse. And while the bill failed in the end due to opposition from conservative women who argued that it would disadvantage housewives (their propaganda suggested that "equal rights" would make mothers eligible for subscription to the armed forces, for example[ll]), the genie was well and truly out of the bottle: women had glimpsed *freedom* on the horizon, and there would be no looking back.

But there was a long way to go. The year 1976 also saw the publication of both Adrienne Rich's *Of Woman Born* and Nancy Felipe Russo's American Psychological Association paper on "The Motherhood Mandate." Both Rich and Russo sought to expose the "unexamined assumptions" (as Rich phrased it) of what was coming to be understood as the patriarchal institution of motherhood—within which childrearing had come to be seen as the only valid life-path for women. Their work showed how, in severely restricting women's influence beyond the home, motherhood being positioned this way also limited women's ability to weave their stories, opinions, needs, and desires into the fabric of public life. Let alone economic policy. But at that point, the notion that to be a woman was to be a mother was still deeply entrenched. As Russo noted, "Characterizing motherhood as prescribed . . . does not adequately communicate the centrality of this behavior to the adult female. . . . It is a woman's raison d'etre. It is mandatory."

This was the case for our mothers, for their mothers, and for their mothers before them. But for the *new* generation now coming through, the concept of a woman's right to self-authorship, and to an identity and a purpose beyond motherhood, was circulating in the air we gulped down with our first breaths. To whatever degree our mothers were involved with or identified with the message of second-wave feminism (and whatever the failings of the movement, which we will examine elsewhere), we were the first generation to have internalized *from birth* that the Motherhood Mandate was ours to overturn. As such, the very mother's milk that nurtured us was infused with the taste of *revolution*. For girls raised against this backdrop, "radical" feminist ideas from the 1970s, 1980s, and 1990s are not only commonplace but have come to be seen as *common sense*. Like, *of course* a woman should be able to live her life as whomever the fuck she wants to be—a message that has intensified for each new delivery of girl babies to be born since. Girl babies who, naturally, have grown up to pursue all sorts of dreams, vocations, and career paths besides motherhood. The logical conclusion of this being what the 2020 US Census revealed as the steepest drop-off in the birth rate since World War II.

But so ancient, so sticky, and so emotionally charged is the conditioned belief that no woman is complete until she has a child, it's like the culture at large still hasn't caught up. The fact that abortion access is being rolled back again in the United States at the time of writing shows the extent to which the notion that "women are mothers" is stuck playing on repeat, in the same way as "men go to war" and "cows are for milking" (when, clearly, in the 2020s, war is a barbaric and ludicrously costly endeavor, and we should really all be vegan). As recently as 2015, Orna Donath noted in *Regretting Motherhood* that "an early desire for non-motherhood is seen as *the* primary deviation a girl can take from her path towards becoming a socially acceptable woman, and it is often thought to be something that will change, or align, with time."

Essential to the upholding of the gendered status quo, pronatalism continues to dictate that mother, and thus homemaker, is a woman's only acceptable role—helping to insure male dominance outside the home in business, politics, finance, and the arts. Not to mention that the capitalist economic system still relies on women's unpaid childrearing labor. Meanwhile, pronatalism also *requires* the continued stigmatization of non-mothers. Intense feelings of shame about being a woman without kids, the notion that this makes her a *selfish cunt*, a sense that she is missing out, and fears about growing old alone if she doesn't become a mom all help to deter women from pursuing the other, potentially disruptive paths that have been made available to us.

And as long as non-moms continue to be seen as selfish, lonely, deviant, or defective, women will be corralled into the opposite: a motherhood mandate that demands a woman's primary focus, *her raison d'etre*, be the birthing, nurturing, and raising of her children (often in *addition* to everything else she is now supposed to do and be). The irony being, as Rich also points out, that "it is precisely the institution of motherhood which . . . has influenced women against becoming mothers. It is simply too hypocritical, too exploitative of mothers and children, too oppressive." Seen this way, not having kids is perhaps the definitive way for a woman to throw off the shackles of patriarchy. The big reveal being that as the final Gen X holdouts surface from our middle forties without mini-me's in tow, we are often not nearly so regretful and unfulfilled as predicted. We have also embarked on all sorts of adventures, and lived to tell all sorts of tales, that we might never have been able to aspire to had we also had kids. As such, a new picture—and a new phase in the evolution of womankind—is emerging.

* * *

In "The Motherhood Mandate," Russo points to the importance of role models in establishing "sex-role stereotypes," noting that (in 1976), "Models [for women] provided in school, in the media, and in books, tend to reinforce the high visibility of motherhood." But by the time Madonna's Susan character sashayed into my life just a decade later, this was changing rapidly. Fast-forward to today, and while Russo's sex-role stereotypes still exist, they often feel as dated as the notion that men are from Mars and women are from Venus.

When I consider what I internalized from the wider culture about what it meant to "be a woman," what arises is a mixed bag that's as colorful, as curious, and as unique as the tangle of tatty costumes in my childhood dress-up chest. Being a woman meant so much more than being "a mom" (even if this remained a baseline requirement). It meant walking to work in sneakers, then switching them for heels. It meant Campari sodas, glamorous dresses, and big hair. It meant being the Iron Lady who everybody hated. It meant spreading your legs in the pages of *Playboy* magazine. And then there was Dad's new girlfriend and her twin sister, both of whom had office jobs, always wore lipstick, and told us stories about serving up cheese fondue and going clubbing with their guests when they worked as chalet girls at a fancy ski resort.

What did becoming "a woman" mean to you when you were young, and how did your family of origin, and your social and cultural background, influence this? What did you learn about what it meant to be "female" or "feminine" growing up? Did this line up with how you felt about yourself? In my case, like so many women, I learned to equate femininity with physical attractiveness, and in the culture that I was raised in, "being pretty" was very much synonymous with being thin. Books, movies, and TV shows also instilled in me the primacy of finding "the one" (and "he" had better be tall, handsome, and, ideally, rich). But at the same time, neither of my parents ever suggested that marriage or motherhood were things they expected of me—an attitude that deviates from the norm, and which undoubtedly helped me claim my Affirmative No early on. All they wanted, they said, was for me to be *happy* when I grew up—but it was never implied that I would arrive at this mythical state as the result of my having a child of my own.

That said, when I first told my dad I had no plans to have kids, his melodramatic response was, "Ah, then you'll never know what *real love* is." But this was odd, given that his definition of paternal love included long periods of time when it felt to me like he'd forgotten I existed. It was his melancholic advice that I shouldn't ever worry about getting married, delivered weary and teary-eyed when I was around age eight and he and Mum were in the final throes of their separation, that landed with the resonance of truth.

Growing up to be married without kids, I inadvertently took the *opposite* of his advice. And in some ways, this has left me free to pursue the life he actually modeled for me with his actions. A woman's mother used to be her first and most vivid role model, but many women without kids are more our fathers' daughters. After all, it often looked like the better deal—didn't it? Not all of our fathers have made the best role models in terms of their life choices, but while my mum remained tethered to the stove while struggling to earn enough to make ends meet (she did her therapy training once my brother and I had both left home), my father had always been free to travel, and write, and teach. Speaking on a podcast on the subject of women's ambition, forty-seven-year-old law professor and author (and mother of two) Lara Bazelon echoed this sentiment when she noted: "My dad was gone a great deal traveling for work while I was growing up, and I think I realized I didn't want [my mom's] constraints; I wanted his freedom. He was able to pursue his ambition and do what he wanted."

In some ways, this speaks to the blurring of the gender binary that began in the 1960s, while it dovetails with current, radical progress in the realm of gender and biological sex. In the Merriam-Webster dictionary, gender is defined as "the behavioral, cultural, or psychological traits typically associated with one sex." But note the use of the word "typically": in the hyper-progressive internet era, nothing about the world we are living in today is typical of what has come before. Including the role models any person, regardless of their biology, might aspire to. So, what if we saw the patriarchal "mother" figure simply as its own distinct *gender role*? One that denotes a specific set of "behavioral, cultural, and psychological traits" that are not limited to biological women—and that equally, not all those born with the physical capacity for birthing life are destined to embody.

After all, in *Regretting Motherhood* Orna Donath notes, "Some women in my study also related to their former selves [as non-mothers] as being comparatively genderless, because they largely felt they had the ability to do what they wanted without being aware of any 'inferiority' due to femininity. . . . Motherhood awoke in them a feeling of being drenched in feminine gender, without the freedom to roam the earth as though they were free of it." This was the relatively genderless "freedom" that I saw embodied in the Susan character—which may feel more like a *loss* of her feminine identity to a woman who always imagined she would be a mom, and for whom it hasn't happened. As a woman without kids, have you ever felt less "feminine" than other adult females?

Women without kids are sometimes made to feel we are "defective," while in reality our lives often more closely resemble the masculine "ideal" (masculinity automatically seen as better under patriarchy). Meanwhile, the all-pervasive Mommy Binary, where "freakish" women without kids are pitted against "natural" women who have fulfilled their maternal duty, only serves to reinforce the gendered status quo.

All binary "either/or" thinking perpetuates oppressive hierarchies: with each polarity perceived as mutually exclusive, one is inevitably positioned as superior or more desirable than the other. But in this case, the Mommy Binary presents a double-bind, since, according to Adrienne Rich, "whichever we did has been turned against us." Under patriarchy, motherhood is equated with servitude, while becoming "a mom" curtails a woman's ability to express every aspect of who she is. Get "unlucky" or opt out, on the other hand, and you are destined to die alone and unloved. Both assessments conjure two-dimensional caricatures of what it actually means to be a woman. To be a human being, parent or not.

Binary thinking dehumanizes all beings as it erases the vast and complex diversity of human experience. And in some ways, modern moms *are* granted a degree of both/and flexibility: a mother is allowed to love her kids more than life itself AND to acknowledge that being a mom can be sheer thankless drudgery. But non-moms still tend to exist in the two-dimensional, either/or space: we are either grieving something we never even had the chance to hold OR we are cold-hearted, delusional, and self-obsessed. Through a nonbinary lens, however, we see that both motherhood and non-motherhood may be experienced in a multitude of ways and subject to a full spectrum of opinions, projections, and conflicted feeling states.

This idea forms the basis of clinical psychologist Aurélie Athan's research in the emerging field of "reproductive identity," which posits that how we choose to express our reproductive potential should be an identity category in its own right. Athan's 2020 paper on the subject frames reproduction as "a healthy aspect of human expression to be openly explored, destigmatized, and self-authored." As with sexuality and gender, Athan argues, an individual's relationship to their *reproductive orientation* is integral to the formation of an authentic self.

For example, choosing to identify as either "childless" (can't have kids) or "childfree" (don't want kids) helps people communicate their reproductive status as women without kids to others. This binary has already been expanded to include terms such as "childless-by-circumstance" and "childfree-after-infertility," which get deeper into the nuance. In my case, I've been experimenting with the term "a-reproductive." Like "a-sexual," to me this denotes my experience of never having had any desire to reproduce. I didn't choose to be childfree. To me, it feels like I was born this way.

As for what's "normal"? When it comes to the realization of their reproductive intentions (the decision whether to have kids, how to parent, with whom, and under what circumstances), Athan's research has found that "males and females of all ages and sexual orientations are inconsistent when it comes to their attitudes, decisions . . . and practices." This suggests that "the nature of reproductive intention is genuine uncertainty. Relatively few people hold strong and unequivocal beliefs, and instead, typically fall somewhere in the middle, are ambivalent, or even indifferent." How does the notion that our reproductive identity can be both fluid and non-gender-specific land with you? How does it impact your assessment of where you orient on the Motherhood Spectrum?

Athan's work pays tribute to pioneers in the realm of psychosocial identity formation—those brave outliers who have helped to reshape society as we know it by demanding greater representation for groups who have been marginalized and oppressed based on race, sexuality, gender, and disability (four of the "Big Eight" social identifiers that also include age, ethnicity, religion, and socioeconomic status). Her assessment that a person's reproductive life is not only influenced by all of the above but also deserves to be considered as an identity category in its own right shows just how far we've come since Russo's observation in "The Motherhood Mandate" that "for many females [and males] the idea of a woman being something other than primarily mother and wife has been literally unthinkable—a 'nonconscious ideology.'"

In the previous chapter, we looked at how our healing and personal evolution happens when we are able to bring to consciousness that which has been unconscious. No longer held hostage by conditioned beliefs and responses that play on autopilot, we are able to reclaim our agency over how our lives play out. In debunking the notion of the Mommy Binary and asking us to confront the conditioning around gender that equates womanhood with motherhood, Athan's work helps us do exactly this. As such, the concept of reproductive identity has huge potential for easing the cognitive dissonance experienced by so many emancipated, twenty-first-century women; that is, for healing the schism that exists between the assumption that motherhood is our calling, and an equally profound pull to be the authors of own destiny.

* * *

When I decided at age nine that I was ready to be a woman, what I really wanted was the freedom to be *me*. The way I saw it, adulthood would bring the freedom to live how I wanted, and to prioritize my own needs without feeling guilty about it. But if anything, the feelings of not "fitting in" that had colored my childhood only intensified as my physical self matured. I was late to develop breasts, and my period lagged behind the other girls'; while they morphed into ready-made mini-women, smoking and flirting, hair falling in perfect flicks, I remained suspended in a spongy in-between. What had I missed? I'd expected my teens to bring self-confidence and autonomy, but the rules of the adult world felt excluding and undecipherable.

The decades passed, and I found new ways to shape and mold myself into the woman I thought I was supposed to be. The right clothes, the right job, the right body shape. But by the time I was in my thirties, my non-mom status meant I often felt an outgrown version of that same awkward teenager. Especially when I was around my mom friends. While they got to grips with feeding schedules and school catchment zones, I was still grappling with my existential angst, partying too much and obsessing over my career. I began to wonder: *If I didn't have kids myself, would I ever really grow up?* It was clear, as Jean Veevers notes in her 1980 book *Childless by Choice* (she coined the term) that "[in the eyes of society] anybody who accepts the 'parenthood prescription' joins the ranks of the mature, the secure, the respectable, and the adult." Is there a part of you that feels immature or underdeveloped as a woman without kids? If so, how has this impacted your self-image?

Aurélie Athan came to her theories about reproductive identity via her other area of research: a concept known as "matrescence." "Matrescence like adolescence," she told me when I interviewed her for this book. That is, the developmental phase that occurs as women transition from non-motherhood to motherhood. The concept was first introduced by medical anthropologist and breastfeeding advocate Dana Raphael in 1975. Raphael identified matrescence as a time in a woman's life, especially if she has experienced a high level of personal autonomy prior to becoming a mom, that is often marked with feelings of distress and disenchantment—not unlike those experienced by young people as they undergo the hormonal changes of adolescence while being confronted with the responsibilities and the injustices of the adult world. The concept has helped destigmatize postpartum depression while also making it easier for women to secure the support needed in order to experience what Athan calls "postpartum flourishing."

But the same way completing an MBA doesn't make anybody a millionaire entrepreneur overnight, becoming a parent does not automatically "grow a person up." It is in fact only one of a multitude of life experiences that can help a person transition to our mature adult self. When non-moms are branded "immature," it's not because we've skipped a developmental stage physically. Physical maturation is a given, and it will continue without any effort on our part until the day we die. And while the experience of gestating, birthing, and nursing a child takes its toll on a woman's body, it does not necessarily "age" her physically. No. When society deems women without kids as remaining childish ourselves, it is a comment on our perceived emotional and psychological immaturity.

But we essentially mature emotionally any time we are forced to grapple with what are the central conflicts of our humanity: the facts that we all make mistakes, that sometimes what's best for us is not so great for others, that the universe *does* play favorites, and that some degree of suffering is unavoidable. As such, we display emotional maturity when we're able to own our choices, including the bad ones; when we don't run from uncomfortable emotions; when we do the right thing versus the easy thing; and when we're able to be vulnerable and reveal our perceived flaws. This is not the same as the "stiff upper lip" mentality of older generations, where any display of emotion was seen as childish. If anything, emotional maturity is the result of learning to express our full range of emotions in a healthy way.

And yes, a toddler's stage-three meltdown at the supermarket checkout may well force a person to "woman-up." Having a kid can be a fast-track to a fortifying dose of existential suffering—bringing a person, as it inevitably does, face-to-face with one's own limitations and perceived failures, not to mention the over-all injustice of the world. When I consider how it must feel to have to explain racism, homophobia, homelessness, or climate change to one's child, the shattering of innocence is enough to make me want to weep. This alone has been a factor in my decision not to have kids.

But still, becoming a mom does not equip a person to grow from the experience in and of itself. In fact, there are plenty of emotionally *immature* parents in the world—the impact of growing up in such a household often leading to what clinical psychologist Lindsay Gibson describes as "lingering feelings of anger, loneliness, betrayal, or abandonment." This is because "emotionally immature parents . . . use coping mechanisms that resist reality rather than dealing with it. They don't welcome self-reflection, so they rarely accept blame or apologize . . . and they're blind to their children's needs once their own agenda comes into play." Emotionally mature parenting, on the other hand, means not projecting your emotional state onto your kids or being triggered by their emotional outbursts—something that may not come so naturally if one is still carrying the unconscious wounds and dysfunctional emotional inheritance of one's own childhood.

Meanwhile, automatically labeling non-mothers as immature assumes that we have not *lived*. But every woman without kids will have experienced her share of setbacks and disappointments; will have felt invisible to somebody we love; will have been unfairly discriminated against; will have had to fake it 'til we make it, or grieve a loss, or pretend we're not hurting when our insides feel like they've been stripped from our body and laid across hot coals. Will have not got something that we've wanted with every cell in our beings. We grow the fuck up emotionally when we are able to confront the traumas and the losses and the unfairness of life head-on. What experiences have helped you mature emotionally, and what was it about them that helped to "grow you up"? And if motherhood is not a prerequisite for maturity, what does being a mature woman mean and look like to you?

If anything, going against the grain and staying true to what you believe is right for you, especially when everyone around you insists that this means *there is something wrong with you*, is one of the surest ways to mature emotionally as a human being. Pushing back and questioning the status quo is part of growing up—it's why teenagers rebel! As is being forced to take a path you never would have chosen but that has chosen you (as for the involuntarily childless). Each requires a person to become intimately familiar with what they believe, what they need, and what makes life meaningful to them. It means being in touch with and accepting desires and aspirations for oneself that may be seen as deviant, and grappling with the guilt, shame, and ostracization that sometimes accompanies this.

And if our unconventional path draws criticism, this in turn means committing to radical self-love and establishing one's own code of ethics while seeking fulfillment and a sense of purpose outside of the tidy parameters of what is deemed socially accept-able. This process will be familiar to anybody who has ever experienced being othered—or even persecuted—whether due to race, religion, sexuality, gender expression, disability, or class. Or for being single, for getting a divorce, for having an abortion, or for *being a less than perfectly selfless mom*. All experiences that require a person, first and foremost, to uncover and advocate for *who we are* and *what we need*, no matter what our family, our culture, or society at large has got to say about it.

Before any girl becomes a mother, first she is a woman. And while matrescence speaks to the process of "growing into" motherhood, what if being a woman without kids simply means becoming more of who she's always been, and already is? What if there were no pre-prescribed rules for what it meant to be a "woman," mother or not? Who would we be growing into then?

"

"I married a Mormon at age nineteen, and he wanted to get me pregnant immediately. I woke up one day and realized, 'I don't belong here.' I had dreams of going to college and wasn't ready for kids, so I left him after only a year of marriage. It was a very arduous journey for a twenty-year-old, before cell phones, living a twenty-four-hour drive away from my home state."

— **age forty-one, single**

"I had my fallopian tubes removed in my late thirties, and while I knew in my heart that I just didn't want to have children, [it] was surprisingly heavy. I didn't change my mind, and I have zero regrets about getting fixed, but I remember really thinking about it as I was preparing for surgery, just because I knew it would be a final, final decision at that point."

— **age forty, single**

"Unfortunately, anything that centers women as humans instead of sex objects or mothers is inherently feminist."

— **age thirty-six, in a domestic partnership**

"

CHAPTER 4

Sexual
Evolution

"ONE, TWO, THREE, FOUR, FIVE *beeeaaaauuuutiful ladies!*"
The men picked us out one by one with their chant, which followed
us along the cobbled streets of Amsterdam's Red-Light District.
The windows of the storefronts were stacked with rainbow-colored
bongs, some showcasing live women writhing in leopard-print
underwear. Reflected in the glass, we five "ladies" shimmered in
the melting midsummer heat, on a summer break to the city famed
for its lax marijuana laws and relaxed attitude to sex work. *Without
our parents.* Our mothers had come to see us off as we'd boarded
the overnight coach at Victoria Bus Station, wearing anxious smiles,
arms crossed tight over their chests. We were sixteen years old: sen-
sible, mature, intelligent young women, they'd reassured each other
with their eyes, their faces sickly yellow in the jaundiced nighttime
light of the bus depot. *We'd be fine.*

Striding the summer streets five-abreast in our short shorts
and cropped tops, I knew I should be annoyed with the men
who lurked along the sidewalks, eating up our tender thighs
and exposed midriffs with their eyes. But instead, the attention
felt like confirmation that I was indeed a beautiful, sexy *woman*,

like the ones dancing in the windows. A straight-A student, my acute shyness meant I was flunking in what had swiftly become the most important area of study: *boys*. Which may have been why, on the last day of our trip, I said yes to the man with the leather jacket and the long Jesus hair when he turned over a beer coaster at the Bulldog Café, wrote my name on it, and told me to give him my number.

We'd been gathered, giggling, in a store, selecting packs of novelty rolling papers as souvenirs, when he'd bowled over and cut the vibe dead: *Awww, look at the tourists*. But he and his friend were from London too, and they were also heading back that night. When he'd invited us to come for one last smoke, he'd somehow positioned it as something we owed him for the attention he'd paid us. At the coffee shop, he rolled joint after joint, his eyes slyly scanning my hair, my face, resting on my dusky pink hotpants. I felt hot and exposed; for some reason he'd picked *me*. The weed was so strong that it made me forget how to speak, and I'd been too dazed to write down any other digits than those that would connect him directly to my mother's home telephone.

By the time I got back home he'd already left a message on the answering machine. My mum was spooked by the fact that he was twenty-two; I shrugged it off, but the sound of his voice made my insides clench up, too. Something about him repulsed me. But his cocky self-confidence also made it hard for me to say no when he told me he would be taking me out that weekend. The first time we had sex, we were in his bedroom at his parents' house, the chintzy floral wallpaper and pastel sheets clashing with the *Scarface* poster and the baseball bat he slept with under the bed. He pursed his thin lips in displeasure when I told him I'd done it before; his name was *Adam*, and I got the impression he liked the idea of being my first man. He also knew I was on the pill, which I'd started taking the year before. But since I didn't know how to explain that I'd actually only done it *one* other time, I didn't. In fact, I didn't say anything, until afterwards when he asked me: "did you come?" "Uh-huh," I lied, sitting up and attempting a smile as I pulled the covers over my naked form, before taking a drag on the joint he'd rolled for me. Part of me would remain there, fake smile frozen on my face, for the duration of our six-year relationship.

Was this not how I was supposed to have responded? All I'd learned about sex in school was how babies were made and how not to get pregnant. The logistics and the efficacy of various forms of contraception, and the names and symptoms of the different STDs. The female orgasm had most definitely not been part of the curriculum, the female orgasm being surplus to reproductive requirements. Since sex was primarily for procreation, and since boys *had* to ejaculate to make a baby, male orgasm was positioned as a biological *need*.

As for instructions on deciding who to have sex with and how to negotiate who did what to whom, these I'd had to cobble together from movies, *Seventeen* magazine, and Jilly Cooper novels, all of which implied that since men *only want one thing*, they had better want *me*.

The underlying message (as in unconscious, and therefore all-powerful) being that a woman being wanted, taken, owned, and ultimately impregnated (by the right person, at the right time) was the natural order of things. And deeply interwoven with *this* was the notion that men (and society) were essentially entitled to women's bodies as the means of reproduction. Part and parcel of Russo's Motherhood Mandate, my friends and I had been subtly indoctrinated from an early age to believe that our raison d'etre was, in fact, to be *fuckable*—as in knock-up-able. A message that was as old as patriarchy—and one that the 1990s sex-positive feminist movement had attempted to turn on its head.

By the time I moved in with Adam at age eighteen, the empowered thing now was for women to have sex "like men." That is, freely, frequently, and for our physical gratification first and foremost. Forget making babies. For men, sex had always been about pleasure, with none of the consequences of pregnancy. Now, as sexually liberated women, we were entitled to the same. Within this context, being down to fuck was not a sign of submissiveness but a way for women to own our sexuality.

But as freeing and empowering as this sentiment might appear on the surface, it simply mimics the most cartoonish version of the masculine libido. That is, one rooted in entitlement, and which glosses over things such as emotional intimacy and mutual consent. The only "pleasure" I got from my encounters with Adam was the fleeting validation of feeling wanted. Meanwhile, for all the advances of the sex-positivity movement, the pressure for women to put our cunts to "proper" use *eventually* is still very much alive beneath the surface, while high rates of sexual violence against women, a resurgence of misogynistic rhetoric online, and regressive anti-abortion laws reflect a vicious backlash to women having more say over our sexual lives.

Within this, we see the unfinished work of the sexual revolution, which is to eradicate any and ALL expectations about our sexual expression, regardless of gender, including what we do and don't desire, who we have sex with and why, and the role sex plays in our lives. What does being "sexually liberated" mean to you, and why? As I see it, "owning one's sexuality" might mean having lots of sex, and it might mean having none at all. It most definitely means the freedom to self-determine when it comes to one's reproductive identity. The role of women without kids within this? To live unapologetically in defiance of centuries-old conditioning about who were are as sexual beings—so as to set a living, breathing example of true sexual liberation for generations to come.

* * *

If the twentieth century saw the unfolding of the sexual revolution, then in the 2020s the time is ripe for sexual *evolution*—that is, a total reimagining of our sexual selves, and a mass departure from the overarching narrative that has defined human sexuality to date. Symbolically speaking, by revoking the biological imperative to procreate, women without kids are the walking, talking embodiment of this; "proof" that women's bodies and sexuality are not inextricable from the procreative project. And as long as we are seen as deviant and "unnatural," and as long as women who can't get pregnant are deemed as having "failed," we will know there is still work to be done.

After all, historically it has been natal women who have (literally and unfairly) borne the consequences of sex. It is women who become pregnant; women who gestate the developing fetus; women whose bodies are split in two by the agony of childbirth; and (even in the most progressive families) women who must put everything else on pause in order to nurture the infant after it is born. This is why the advent of effective birth control and safe, legal abortion have been central to the sexual revolution. A movement that has essentially sought to free women from the burdens of reproduction—enabling us to choose when and with whom to have kids, and to prioritize our own freedom and well-being, sexual and otherwise.

The sexual revolution has also manifested in the destigmatization of self-pleasure and sex before marriage, advances in LGBTQIA+ rights, and a push to decriminalize sex work. Within this, sex for pleasure, intimacy, and personal empowerment has been framed as equally valid as sex for reproductive purposes. Meanwhile, the less *sexy* parts of the sexual revolution could also be said to include calls for paid parental leave and universal childcare, which equally help to "free" women to be sexual without fear of the potential consequences: the career setbacks, stigma, and financial instability inherent in unplanned parenthood.

In some ways, the rising number of women without kids can be read as a natural by-product of the sexual revolution; the birth rate began to decline steeply in 1965, following the introduction of oral contraceptives. But the slippery sheath of *shame* that we still often inhabit, the gossipy side-eye and the overall distaste that we are subject to, tells me that society at-large can still only *really* stomach women's sexuality when it is employed in service of a specific role: that of "respectable" wife and mother. If you're reading this, you've felt it: any woman who remains freely sexual without eventually assuming this role is still viewed with suspicion.

We like to think our ideas about human sexuality have evolved, but in many ways we're stuck in the dark ages with this subject, forever falling backward down potholes on the road to enlightenment. We see this in the rolling back of *Roe v. Wade*, which, lurking behind the pro-life rhetoric, seems to want to punish women for having sex for sex's sake. We see it in the tabloid vilification of "other" women, the harlots and the homewreckers. We see it in acts of homophobia and transphobia, since queer sex, generally speaking, flies a rainbow flag in the face of baby-making sex. And we also see what is the underlying dogma of heteropatriarchy— *men's entitlement to women's bodies as the means of reproduction*—in the pervasive influence of the male gaze, in incidents of sexual and domestic violence against women, and in the misogynistic views of the incel (involuntary celibate) movement. Not to mention in predatory older guys claiming ownership of younger women's bodies, and naive girls like me *just going along with it*.

All of which boils down to quite the witches' brew.

The toxicity of this became clear when I was considering calling this book *Selfish Cunt*. This book *wanted* to be called *Selfish Cunt*; the title pulsed in my brain like a horny teenager while I was working on my proposal. I mean, isn't the whole point of women's sexual liberation to be *selfish* about what we do with our *cunts*? But when I reached out to people about conducting research interviews, I shied away from it, subbing in the softer *Women Without Kids*. Not being able to say the *c*-word out loud would definitely be an issue when it came to selling books. Unlike with the *f*-word—there having been a moment there when putting "Fuck" in your book title practically guaranteed a bestseller. But while we're apparently fine with fucking, the fact that the word *cunt* is so reviled shows just how much pain, fear, and loathing still exists in the realm of female sexuality. That is, how many generations of conditioning about women's sexual submissiveness is stored in our cells; how much shame we harbor about expressing our complex and nuanced sexual selves; and how much sexual trauma, pain, and abuse must be acknowledged, felt, and processed if we want to be free of this in our lifetimes.

By a raise of hands, who here can relate to faking an orgasm, holding back from expressing what you want in bed, or going along with a sexual act when you didn't really want to? Who here has felt the fear vibrating in your chest walking home alone along a darkened street? We didn't need the #MeToo movement to tell us how many of us have experienced some degree of sexual trauma as a result of the inherited (*vs. inherent*) sexual entitlement among men—sexual trauma that was also part of our mothers' and our grandmothers' lived experience, and which has been handed down to us in our DNA. This sexual trauma equally exists in the collective unconscious, where it will remain, manifesting in our default beliefs and behaviors around our sexuality until we consciously choose to disrupt them.

The desire to engage with this work, so that we might finally evolve beyond this, is beginning to be expressed among younger generations. There's the fact that Gen Zs and millennials are having significantly less sex than their predecessors. Sometimes referred to as a "sex recession," this might not actually be a bad thing if it means people are having less unwanted sex. Then there is the steep drop-off in teen pregnancies, concerns about the psychological impact of porn, and current ultra-progressive conversations about gender and biological sex. Taken together, the overarching theme of our emerging sexual landscape is one of discernment, self-determination, and the debunking of stereotypes. If anything, we are witnessing what can feel like a bid to remake human sexuality from the ground up, an observation that extends to the more radical faction of the childfree movement. Reporting on this phenomenon in 2021, Suzy Weiss interviewed several women aged nineteen to thirty-one who had opted for a *laparoscopic bilateral salpingectomy* (known as "The Operation" on childfree Reddit forums)—that is, an irreversible sterilization procedure. Their reasons? Everything from economic instability to climate change to not wanting to raise a kid in a violently racist world.

Having one's tubes not tied but *removed* at age nineteen might seem extreme. But if anything, these outliers are enacting a privilege our foremothers fought long and hard for: the right to self-determine when it comes to our sexual and reproductive lives. A fight that is ongoing; unsurprisingly, requests for The Operation have increased since the overturning of *Roe v. Wade*. And they are equally acting on information that once seemed radical—and which can now simply be taken as fact: that women will never be truly equal to men until, like men, our sexuality is not ultimately seen as a means to a reproductive end.

In many ways, being a woman without kids represents the apex of the feminist dream. So why are we not celebrated for being the torchbearers for sexual and gender equality that we are?

The answer lies again in the pronatalist ideology that perpetuates the gendered sexual binary: the one where men do the fighting and the fucking, and women do the birthing and the nurturing. In the shadowy corners of this binary lie the roots of misogyny—which is at the heart of all gender inequity and all sexual violence toward women and queer and nonbinary people. Defining individuals by their reproductive parts also negates the concept of a human sexuality that is equally about self-expression, personal power, and the giving and receiving of mutual pleasure. And it is deeply entrenched in the collective psyche.

Of course, the past half-century has seen major advances in women's sexual liberation, with many of those leading the charge having been women without kids themselves: women like Shere Hite, whose 1976 *The Hite Report* introduced the clitoris to the masses and proved that the majority of women do not orgasm from intercourse (i.e., baby-making sex)—and whose work drew so much criticism in the United States that she self-exiled to Europe; Betty Dodson, the pro-sex feminist who brought her assistant to orgasm on camera on an episode of Netflix's *The Goop Lab* at age ninety; and prostitute and porn star turned radical sex educator Annie Sprinkle, who has spearheaded the feminist porn movement.

But sexual liberation is not the same as *sexual healing*—and the former cannot come fully into its flourishing without the latter. Sexual healing often begins and ends with healing from the physical and psychological residues of misogyny, while sexual liberation without sexual healing finds us engaging with our sexuality in dysfunctional ways. When I gave Adam unrestricted access to my body, like I was a human ATM, I thought I was being sexually liberated; in reality, I was acting in a scene straight out of the same old patriarchal playbook.

The legacy of our shared ancestry means that everybody and *every body*—including heterosexual, cis male bodies, whose desires have also been perverted and exploited by heteropatriarchy—has sexual healing to do. But the solution is not to say, "Oh look, women's bodies can be just for sex, too." The solution is to teach all people about the true meaning of sexual autonomy—something that is intrinsic to the rising ranks of women without kids.

Forgoing motherhood, for whatever reason, and however we feel about this, means experiencing one's sexuality as separate from its biological function. What surfaces for you when you feel into this? If there were no risk of becoming pregnant or experiencing sexual assault, and no expectation for you to behave a certain way, how would you engage with your sexuality then? Meanwhile, more of us engaging with this work is how we will continue to enact our ongoing sexual *evolution*. For ourselves, of course, but also on behalf of all those women whose bodies are not their own, and who are still being exploited for their sexuality and their reproductive capacity.

* * *

So, what does sexual healing look like in our lives, and how can we engage with it on a personal and a collective level? While it's important for there to be sex-positive expressions of female and queer sexuality, healing our individual and collective sexual wounds is equally a private and *internal* process of recovering the sexual selves that exist beyond prescribed gendered sex roles. The practicalities of this will be individual to each of us—but it begins with understanding why we needed the "sexual revolution" in the first place, the better to understand what we are healing *from*.

The concept of the sexual revolution was first introduced by Austrian psychoanalyst Wilhelm Reich. A protégé of Sigmund Freud, Reich believed that all neurosis and misery was the result of people being severed from their "orgastic potency"—that is, the life force energy of unrestrained pleasure and fulfillment that we experience in orgasm. This severing, he posited, could be traced back to fearmongering religious and political doctrines and oppressive socioeconomic conditions. Religious doctrine often positions pleasure and personal fulfilment (sexual and otherwise) as sinful, while under extractive capitalism these things are only attainable through hard work and consumerism.

In his 1933 classic, *The Mass Psychology of Fascism*, Reich introduced the idea that sexual suppression is part and parcel of fascist ideology—since any *self*-generated feelings of desire, pleasure, and fulfillment that connect us to our individual agency and power pose a threat to existing power structures. Meanwhile, in any system of dehumanization, severing people from that most basic human drive—the drive for orgasm—and creating shame around their sexual expression is a powerful tool of oppression. Shame manifests as the idea that "there is something wrong with me," which, in turn, begets the internalized belief that "I deserve to be treated as less than."

Crucial to our conversation here, Reich noted, "The idealization of motherhood is essentially a means of keeping women from developing a sexual consciousness and from breaking through the barriers of sexual repression." When a woman's only valid role is mother, he meant, her sexuality becomes public property—something to be engaged with for the primary purpose of furthering the species—as opposed to something that belongs to *her* to do with as she pleases.

He also wrote that "the very existence of woman as a sexual being would threaten authoritarian ideology; her recognition and social affirmation [by society at large] would mean its collapse." Here, he suggests that women being seen as men's sexual equals (i.e., being allowed a sexuality beyond its reproductive function) would be a fatal blow to the gendered status quo. An idea that is further extrapolated in the 2019 book *Nurturing Our Humanity*, in which social systems scientist Riane Eisler and anthropologist Douglas P. Fry chart the impact of what they refer to as either "domination systems" or "partnership systems" on human development through the ages.

So-called domination systems rely on top-down control of the population and impose rigid hierarchies and ranking. In contrast, partnership systems are predicated on collaboration, and they promote ideals of mutuality, caring, empathy, and creativity. Like Reich, Eisler and Fry argue that "denying women reproductive freedom (by vilifying non-motherhood, for example) is part of a larger fundamentalist political agenda to maintain, or in some cases force a return to, domination systems where both the male head of household and the male head of state have unquestioned control."

This is ultimately the message of fundamentalist religions that condemn all non-procreative sex as sinful (including masturbation, prostitution, queer sex, and sex outside of marriage). In some cultures, these religious rules are enforced with extreme measures, including the "honor killings" of women and girls who bring shame to the family by engaging in queer, premarital, or extramarital sex, or refusing to enter into an arranged marriage. And while these acts are condemned by international civil rights organizations, similarly tyranical attitudes to sex and sexuality simmer close to the surface in secular, Western countries too. Homophobia and transphobia and punitive anti-abortion laws (those that seek to imprison abortion providers, or to try for murder women who get the procedure, for example) all have their roots in the rigid sexual binary as imposed by organized religions.

Stoking unconscious fears about being punished for more fluid expressions of our sexuality, the through line goes something like: color outside the lines of approved gendered sex roles and there will be hell to pay. Literally, in some cases. And I can smell this same fear in the moral judgments that people often project onto women without kids—as with any woman-identified individual whose sexuality is not employed in service of fulfilling our reproductive duty. Can't you?

Putting these puzzle pieces together is the first step to reclaiming our sexuality from this ancient, oppressive narrative—which is right there in our collective origin story: the story of Adam and Eve, the first man and his wayward wife, thrown out of Paradise and condemned to a life of repentance after she succumbs to her desires and takes a bite from Satan's forbidden fruit. "Fruit" which could be read as a metaphor for female orgasm—the ultimate proof, as Shere Hite's work highlighted, that female sexuality is not just for reproduction.

A mythology that has been passed down, woman to woman, *womb to womb*, through the ages, it has always felt ominously prophetic to me that his name was Adam, too—the man I dutifully submitted to, year after year, even when everything in me recoiled from his touch with a silent, shrinking *no*. Afterwards, I would lie staring into the hollow dark, wondering how the fuck this had become my life. But so ingrained in my psyche was the notion that he was, indeed, entitled to my body, and that my pleasure was irrelevant, that it was only decades after I left him that I could recognize this dynamic as abusive.

So this, all of this, is why we needed the sexual revolution. The twentieth-century movement to normalize premarital sex, queer sex, birth control, and abortion at least having acknowledged that human sexuality has many expressions and functions beyond the procreative act. Any woman who has chosen not to have kids, whatever her reasons for this, has been the beneficiary of this work. But the reason we have yet to be truly sexually liberated—let alone sexually healed—is that there is no escaping the story of human evolution. That is, the one that says men are *designed* to impregnate as many women as possible, and that women are *built* to bear these children. *Again, who can argue with nature?* Following this thread to its logical conclusion, some (male) evolutionary psychologists have even argued that rape is a natural consequence of our evolution as a species. In the controversial *A Natural History of Rape*, for example, the authors argue that forced copulation is just another expression of the violent and domineering "survival-of-the-fittest" instinct that informs natural selection. Abhorrent, of course (depending on who you're talking to), but essentially a by-product of the genetic hustle for survival.

But if we accept this theory, then we must also accept that all men are wired for rape—which is the same sort of logic that says all women are wired for child-rearing. Just because you can, doesn't mean you must. Within this evolutionary worldview, there is also no place for women without kids, even if our emergence has been enabled by evolutions in consciousness that have helped to shape societal progress over the course of the past century. As with the female orgasm, *our very existence is an inconvenient reminder that there is more to life, and sex, than the multiplication of the species.* And what about men who don't have children? Well, there's no way to *prove* they haven't sired a child somewhere down the line, what with all the raping and pillaging they're supposed to have been getting up to.

Ugh. I think we can all agree that it's a marker of human progress that we are evolving beyond this thinking. So, if we can accept that it is not in all men's biological makeup to commit acts of sexual assault, why is it still so hard to accept that not all women are biologically compelled to become mothers? If anything, the flourishing of *womankind* (and thus, ultimately, the thriving of the species) is directly linked to women having control of our bodies, our sexuality, and our own reproductive lives. For example, the better educated and more financially independent the female population, the less kids women have overall, preferring to pour more resources into fewer offspring (benefiting said offspring first and foremost) than stretch themselves to breaking point caring for a larger brood. Simply put, the more say we have over how, when, and if we become mothers at all, the better women do, the better our children do, and the better *human beings* do overall. The sexual revolution was one thing—whatever that term means for you. But what if the next stage in our sexual *evolution* was more of us continuing to have fewer kids?

* * *

Of course, there are those who would argue that preventing pregnancy with the use of birth control or abortion "is not natural"—

and therefore not part of human evolution. This mentality might also claim the same of homosexuality. And speaking of evolution, isn't the whole point of the "sex instinct" to get us to produce as many progenies as possible? Not necessarily. Speaking on a program on childlessness on BBC Radio 4, evolutionary biologist Gillian Ragsdale debunked the notion of a biological maternal instinct: "It has never been necessary for any animal—including humans—to set out wanting to have children. What they have to have is a sex drive," she explained —a drive for orgasm being what she meant. After all, all female mammals have a clitoris, the sole purpose of which is to react to sexual stimulation.

When I called to ask her about this, she spelled it out: when rabbits have sex, they are not thinking about creating baby rabbits. And it's the same with us: "If you woke up on a desert island tomorrow, and you had forgotten everything about what it means to be human, you would try to find food and water. You would probably masturbate at some point. But the thought of wanting a child would never even cross your mind."

The human sex drive, then, is less about a specific desire to procreate than it is about simply expressing the orgastic potency inside of us. Which . . . is kind of what we've been taught about men's relationship to sex. Meanwhile, "So long as you're having miscellaneous sex—lots of it and *most of it non procreative* [emphasis mine]—you will have children. When the kids come along, it is very useful if at that point there is a natural urge to look after them," she concluded. I might never have experienced "baby-fever," but this latter part is something I can absolutely relate to—a desire to protect and provide for young humans (ideally) applicable across the gender spectrum.

And how about when babies don't "just happen" as the result of unprotected sex? Anybody who has not been able to become pregnant "the natural way" and seen it as a personal failing may find cold comfort in the 2020 book *Count Down*, in which environmental and reproductive epidemiologist Shanna H. Swan charts the decline of human fertility rates in Western nations over the past four decades. Sperm counts have plummeted by 50 percent since the 1980s, with diminished ovarian reserve (a condition in which the number and quality of a woman's eggs is lower than expected for her age) and risk of miscarriage rising steadily among women of all ages over the same period. Swan describes her doomsday prognosis as being "rotten," "bleak," and "*No bueno!*" She also lays the blame squarely at the feet of environmental factors, showing how everything from the level of microplastics in our food and water supply to the stress of modern life have negatively impacted human fertility.

And in some ways, the above could also be read as part of our evolution as a species, a case of survival-of-the-fittest gone too far. Stay with me on this one. Many of the technological advances filling our skies with smog and clogging our systems with microplastics started life as low-cost/high-convenience innovations to feed, clothe, house, and transport the rising global population. But equally, the way in which they are implemented often reflects the greed and self-serving mindset of those who have made it to *the top of the industrialized food chain*: the corporate "robber-bandits" (in the words of feminist copywriter Kelly Diels) for whom the hoarding of resources is just good business. If anything, Swan's alarmist book is part of a great awakening to all the ways in which our planet, our species, and, as it turns out, our procreative potential have been decimated by the evolution of extractive capitalism. So, what does it mean to have come of age at a time where human beings' biological capacity to reproduce is no longer a given—another important factor in the rising numbers of women without kids?

I believe that we find ourselves right here, right now for a reason. Considering the harm done to our planet and our shared humanity by the domination systems that have shaped modern civilization, what if what the world really *needs* is for us to slow down with the procreation until every adult human has had the opportunity to heal their wounds around sexuality, gender, race, bodily autonomy, power, and spirituality, as inflicted by centuries of dogmatic religious, economic, and social control? Until the non-human world has had a chance to regenerate itself? What if Mother Nature is telling us that it's time to stop *reproducing more of the same* and focus on tending to these collective wounds instead—the same way we are currently tasked with sucking carbon from the skies and cleaning up our oceans? What if boldly claiming your place in the growing movement of women without kids were a vital part of this?

Okay, okay—I appreciate that this is a pretty far-out framing of what could ultimately lead to *the end of the human race!* I also don't mean to minimize the pain of anybody who has experienced fertility issues, or the anxieties of those who have made the difficult choice not to have kids due to fears about the environment. But human beings are nothing if not adaptable: what if the revolutionary rise of women without kids were an evolutionary adaptation to conditions on planet Earth that are simply not supportive of our continued flourishing?

* * *

It is white cis-gendered Western women who have benefitted most from the advances of the sexual revolution. When my mother thought it would be wise for me to go on the pill at age fifteen, it was because the underlying message for girls of my generation was that becoming pregnant too soon (motherhood still being the eventual goal) would mean *game over*. It would mean the end of freedom, the end of opportunity, the end of any chance at a meaningful career. The end of our potential to live as self-actualized, creatively fulfilled, and financially independent women. This message has been powerfully disruptive to the gendered status quo—and it has resulted in more women having fewer kids. But it does not necessarily encompass the notion of liberation and healing, sexual and otherwise, for all.

Within the directive to avoid becoming pregnant at any cost, white women growing up on the heels of women's lib were essentially being groomed to be men's equals in a world created by white men for white men. That is, a world that continues to reward competition, self-sufficiency, and the accumulation of assets. What is not immediately obvious here is that second- and third-wave feminism have unwittingly continued to privilege and exalt the straight, white, masculine ideal. The more closely people of all genders are able to emulate this—for example, by not becoming mothers—the better they will continue to do. When the SisterSong Women of Color Reproductive Justice Collective formed in 1997, the aim was to highlight specific factors negatively impacting the reproductive lives of women of color that were not being addressed by mainstream white feminism: from enforced sterilization and high maternal mortality to difficulty accessing birth support choices and parents being separated from children through racially biased immigration and incarceration practices.

The founders coined the term "reproductive justice" through an amalgamation of "reproductive rights" and "social justice" to describe their aims. This is defined by current executive director Monica Simpson as

> an intersectional framework that advocates for the human right to have the children that we want, to not have children, to end pregnancies, and to have access to the contraceptives that we need to determine how we want to make a family or not. Overall, reproductive justice is about the human right to self-determine, the ability to be able to live free from fear and violence, and to have healthy lives so that we can grow and live into our destinies.

This is a doctrine that could be the manifesto for a truly woman-centric feminism and a *real* sexual revolution: that is, one that serves our ultimate evolution as a species, moving us beyond systems of domination and oppression and toward a more equitable world.

As for what it will really take for us to move beyond ancient narratives about the nature of human sexuality? In the name of leveling the playing field, I can see the benefit of a movement encouraging men to have sex "like women": that is, as if each sexual encounter might result in pregnancy, seriously limiting one's life choices going forward. To this day, I also wonder if things would have gone differently with Adam and me if I'd been taught in school that sex is *primarily* about self-expression, connection, empowerment, self-awareness, intimacy, and trust. Like, what if all new people coming onto the planet learned that instead of sex being part of a contractual agreement as to who owes what to whom, the most important thing of all is to always love yourself? That babies, should parenthood be something a person feels they are cut out for, were just the by-product of an activity to be engaged in primarily for the purpose of *feeling good*. And that in a world of unavoidable suffering, sex is a gift and a reminder that our bodies are built to experience well-being, satisfaction, and joy.

This is the approach sexuality educator Justine Ang Fonte was taking when she was forced to resign from her position at the prestigious Dalton School on the Upper East Side of Manhattan in 2021. All she was trying to teach, she explained when we spoke, was that "until we also understand that sex is about pleasure and power and agency, we cannot understand who we are as sexual beings." This is especially relevant to sex ed classes (which supposedly are about keeping young people safe), as you can't have a real conversation about consent, for example, without talking about what feels good, what doesn't, and why. And you can't talk about these things without talking to kids about intimacy, masturbation, homosexuality, and porn.

Meanwhile, Fonte is also an advocate for teaching about "a gender-full world, rather than a gendered world that limits us to being defined by our reproductive parts." A gender-full world that would also incorporate the concept of the Motherhood Spectrum. She also told me that, given how far we have to go, she does not expect to see a world in which human beings are truly sexually liberated in her lifetime.

In the meantime, a powerful manifesto for the reclamation of the *erotic* beyond the sexual act can be found in adrienne maree brown's *Pleasure Activism*, which positions pleasure as fuel for enacting social justice. Brown quotes Audre Lorde's 1981 *Uses of the Erotic: The Erotic as Power* as what helped her reorient her life, her work, and her activism toward helping all beings experience joy and personal fulfilment: "The erotic is . . . an internal sense of satisfaction to which, once we have experienced it, we can aspire. For having experienced the fullness of this depth of feeling and recognizing its power, in honor and self-respect we can require no less of ourselves," Lorde wrote. Framed this way, acknowledging and embodying the erotic in us—synonymous in many ways with Reich's orgastic potency—means knowing what we want, going after it, and living a life where we feel satisfied on every level, a potent directive for any woman seeking meaning and fulfillment beyond motherhood.

For brown, "Lorde made me look deeply inside my life to find the orgasmic, full-bodied 'yes!' inside of me, inside the communities I love and work with, and inside our species in relationship to our home planet." You've felt that YES, haven't you? It's the kind of yes that won't take no for an answer, the kind of yes that feels like fireworks. She continues: "Once we know the extent to which we are capable of feeling that sense of satisfaction and completion, we can observe which of our various life endeavors brings us closest to that fullness." And for me, brown is writing about the *Affirmative Yes* that has for so long been yoked to motherhood among women, not least by the message that *you will never find fulfillment, or know true love, until you have a child of your own.* It is also the same yes that we clear the way for whenever we are able to find and voice our Affirmative No—about having sex that we don't want, about having kids we are not ready for, or about anything else that is not aligned with our utmost desires for our life.

Which brings to mind something else Gillian Ragsdale had to say, this time about the "feeling rules" attached to motherhood: "Once you have to make rules about something in society, it's a clue that the thing you're trying to inculcate is not natural. All these cultural rules that say women should be married, should have children, you wouldn't need that pressure if women weren't likely to make other choices if they had the freedom." In other words, if our orgasmic, Affirmative Yes wasn't just as likely to take us by the hips and guide us away from the well-tended pastures of motherhood, toward as-yet untraveled pathways to satisfaction, fulfillment, joy, and pleasure for pleasure's sake. Pathways that we are poised to explore together, in sisterhood, as women without kids.

"

"I remember feeling this incredible pressure when I graduated, that within ten years I was supposed to build a career, save for a wedding, get married, pay off student debt, save for a house, save for a kid."

— age forty, about to be divorced

"I had cancer in my early thirties and had to get a hysterectomy. At that time I was not married. As an artist I had not been interested in having a child. It is only now, at age fifty, that I feel settled enough to provide a home for a child. But so far that desire has not been strong enough to lead to me deciding to adopt."

— age fifty, married

"I spent my young childhood in a Catholic and extremely patriarchal society. When my family moved to the US, I felt so much more freedom and possibility in my life and didn't want to let go of that. I feel like having children would rob me of the freedom I love so much."

— age thirty-six, single

"

CHAPTER 5

Enough!

STARING AT THE PALE BLUE LINES on the pregnancy test, I felt a fluttering in my chest like a dandelion being blown to plant a wish. I sat in the cramped, makeshift bathroom my dad had built in a little cupboard in the lower level of his house, where I had been living for the past six months. The chipboard walls felt like they were breathing in time with me, as they emitted their sweet sawdust aroma. Two lines—that meant "pregnant," right? My fingers vibrating lightly, I picked up the box and read the instructions three more times to be sure. Yes, that was correct. I was pregnant.

My first reaction should have been panic; an unintended pregnancy was the equivalent of getting into a ten-car pileup without insurance. But since I already knew I would have an abortion, and since I lived in a country where this service was available free of charge, no questions asked, instead the shot of adrenaline felt light and tingly, like I was coming up on a hit of extremely clean, medical-grade ecstasy. The universe was evidently giving a gigantic thumbs-up to this excellent new person I had met, who was currently waiting for me outside the bathroom reading last month's issue of *The Face*.

I'd come off the pill for good after I left Adam, but it had taken six full months for my hormones to catch up and for me to get my period again. At that point, I'd gone to the Marie Stopes family planning clinic to get myself fitted with an IUD. I'd read that it was the form of birth control favored by female doctors, and supposedly over 99 percent effective. Which felt like some hardcore odds against me finding myself in this situation. Not me: us. My gut performed a slow somersault. Against *us* finding *our*selves in this situation. At twenty-three years old, it was the first time I had been confronted with my Affirmative No about motherhood head-on. There was no question in my mind about what I would do next: there was no way I was having this kid.

It had been less than a year since I'd graduated with a First Class Honors degree in magazine journalism from the London College of Fashion. Within a month of getting my results, I'd packed up my stuff in my little gold Peugeot and told Adam we were done. My degree was the shot of self-esteem I needed to finally find my NO; my ticket to a life that was *all mine*. That fall, my favorite college tutor had taken me for champagne at notorious media haunt the Groucho Club to celebrate my results. "You have a very exciting career ahead of you," he'd told me with a twinkling "cheers!" I would not—*could not*—fuck this up.

All I wanted at that point was a career in magazines. I still couldn't believe I might actually get paid to do something so cool. Making my own money had always been a priority for me, too; I was helping my dad's girlfriend with the filing in her office by age twelve. After Adam and I had moved in together, I'd paid my half of the rent with a job folding sweaters in a store. All I'd wanted *then* was independence, the self-sufficient adult life I'd dreamed of. Coming home to cook him steak and chips, heating a cup of soup for myself, going to college had been an afterthought. But all that was behind me now. I carefully placed the pregnancy test on the arm of the sofa-bed and smiled at the person who already, perplexingly, felt like family to me. With the avenues of possibility lining up in front of me, now I was ready for more.

The abortion itself was uneventful. On the day, both my mother and "the father" accompanied me to the clinic. I was instructed to put on a robe, go to the bathroom, and place a pessary in my vagina, which would help to open up my cervix. Then I was led into an operating room that was lit like midday on the Mediterranean Sea, where I dropped like a stone into the anesthetic blackout. Afterward, there was no blood, no pain, just this lovely man who had taken a whole day off of work to stay with me and take me back to his place, where he propped me up in bed and brought me chocolate and cups of tea. By the next night, I was ready to go out dancing, the whole surreal experience already trailing behind me like the silver string of a sagging helium balloon. Later, twirling under a disco ball to Donna Summer's "I Feel Love," I felt freer, and more thankful for my freedom, than I had ever been.

Terminating a pregnancy is perhaps the ultimate sliding-doors moment, "doors" that open onto very different life-paths, and which, as we have seen, women have only had access to relatively recently. Access that is being rolled back in the United States as I write. Simply put, the fact that there are more women without kids today than at any other time in history reflects more women having more choices as to how our lives play out; apparently, not everybody sees this as a good thing. All the more reason for women without kids to celebrate ourselves and our life choices, and to advocate for every woman, everywhere, to have access to these same choices, too.

Not that the decision not to have a child is always as clear cut as whether or not to have an abortion. Often, it is the result of walking through an interlocking series of doors that it turns out have been leading elsewhere all along. Like one of those choose-your-own-adventure books, where the surprise ending is that you never wound up becoming a mom. So how can we be sure we're knocking on the right doors for us? And what are we opting for instead when the sum of our life choices means we don't have kids?

* * *

My college tutor had been right. Determined to make good on the promise of my degree, it wasn't long before I had wangled my way into the beating heart of the London media machine. It was also during the following decade that the question—*Why don't you want kids?*—would reach fever pitch, coinciding with me scaling what would be the height of my magazine career. All around me, I watched the glossy, ballsy women who had become my peers busily get to work incorporating motherhood into the dossier of achievements they wore like coveted designer labels. Like many of them, my wanting *more* than a life of wifely domesticity had made me unapologetically ambitious. But in my case, knowing I didn't want to be a mom meant I never found myself grappling with how to *have it all.* Three little words that have become synonymous with the six-armed juggle of the upwardly mobile working mother.

A slogan first used by advertisers in the late 1970s, the concept flowered in the public imagination after then-editor of *Cosmopolitan* magazine, Helen Gurley Brown, published her 1982 classic *Having It All: Love, Success, Sex, Money, Even if You're Starting with Nothing.* From this point onward, her title became something of a feminist rallying cry: men had always had it all, now women could have it all too. The irony being that Brown was—wait for it—*a woman without kids!* Yes, you read that correctly. Despite being credited with seeding the idea that mothers could, and should, pursue fulfilling careers and financial independence while also raising kids, children are mentioned just six times in her 492-page book. Reading between the lines, perhaps what she was actually saying—not least by modeling this with her own life—was that it was okay for women to pursue love, success, sex, and money, *and to not be mothers.* That would have been the real feminist slant, so I'll say it here on Brown's behalf: having all the love, success, sex, and money you want, and not feeling like you must also have kids *is okay*! After all, love, success, sex, and money are things that men have been able to pursue freely precisely *because* they are not saddled with the responsibility of childcare.

But this was never going to land in the 1980s. With the patriarchy reeling from the feminist advances of the previous decade, newly minted "career women" were painted as heartless, ball-breaking automatons. That, or dangerously deranged (think Glenn Close's childless publishing exec in the 1987 hit film *Fatal Attraction*). Suggesting that women could succeed in their careers and still be selfless and nurturing softened the blow to the gendered status quo. If anything, the doorway to non-motherhood still wedged stubbornly shut, a woman wanting a career meant she *had to* want it all—since there was *no option* not to also be a mom.

The legacy of this, however, has been the impression that pursuing either one of these life paths to the detriment of the other will never be *enough*. Triggering a case of existential FOMO, in some ways this message is more intense for women without kids. Being a stay-at-home mom may be seen as "playing small," but there's always the sense that a woman is somehow completed by her children. For a woman who chooses her career over having kids, not only is she missing out—something fundamental is missing from her life. Of course, neither scenario is necessarily true. As we've seen, fulfillment comes in many forms, and what makes life meaningful to any one individual will be unique to them. And then there's the fact that very few mortals possess the superpowers (read: time, energy, money, and other resources) necessary to keep all the plates spinning all the time. Meanwhile, attempting to *do it all* often leaves women feeling as if they've failed at both motherhood and in their careers. That they are failing, period.

To the extent that forty years since Brown's book was published, telling women they should have it all no longer feels feminist, it feels sadistic. Especially when the gender pay gap is actually revealed to be the *motherhood* pay gap. Married moms and single moms earn 75 cents and 54 cents respectively on the married male dollar; for women without kids, it's 96 cents.[12] And the moms are the ones with the extra mouths to feed. In reality, it's also not like most mothers—my own included—have had much choice when it comes to earning a wage as well as raising their children. For the majority of families, not only is this expected, it is necessary. Juggling work and family life is not aspirational, it is the norm, *as has always been the case* outside of the heteronormative, white, nuclear family ideal. A norm that also finds many working moms stuck between a rock and very hard place; a place where something—be it one's salary, sleep, sex life, or even sanity—often has to give.

The COVID-19 pandemic only drove this home, when closures of schools and childcare facilities forced women to drop out of the labor force like flies. The house lights thrown unceremoniously on, women's so-called gains in the fight for workplace equality were revealed once and for all to have been little more than a costume, pancake makeup concealing the haggard face of the good old heteropatriarchy. It comes as little surprise that "wine-mom" culture also peaked during the pandemic, which saw a 40 percent increase in problem drinking among women.[13] Feminism had promised freedom; now, stripped of the supports that had enabled that freedom, there was no escaping the oppressive reality of patriarchal motherhood.

Meanwhile, in the 2020s, the notion of even *wanting* it all has come to seem greedy and entitled. *If some people have it ALL (like, say, the billionaires making up the 0.01 percent) then what's left for everybody else?* Not to mention the fact that the outwardly glittering careers of the high-flying *Wikipedia moms*—the ones I find myself comparing my life and achievements to in what feel like acts of emotional self-harm—are often enabled by the women of color making low wages and who make up 45 percent of the childcare economy, a dynamic that some believe has its roots in slavery. Arguing this case in an article on the COVID-19 childcare crisis, president of the Women's National Law Center, Fatima Goss Graves, also pointed out that "everyone and anyone is touched by the need for child-care. Even if you are without children, behind many of your coworkers, nurses, cashiers, Uber drivers, and government workers is the underpaid labor of child-care workers and the unpaid labor of families and friends strung together to make a child-care routine."

A failure to recognize that this is the case was central to billionaire Sheryl Sandberg's 2013 *Lean In* and caused a backlash against the book—a quasi-follow-up to *Having It All* that essentially encouraged women to grit their teeth, buck up, and *suck it up*. This, as opposed to advocating for the things that would actually support working mothers *and their children*, such as more flexible hours, extended periods of paid parental leave, universal healthcare, free childcare, and, not least, an emphasis on reeducating boys and men about the responsibilities of parenthood. But since it is estimated that policies such as these would cost the economy upward of $70 billion per year, and since "mothering" continues to be categorized as a gendered *labor of love*, it is small wonder that the ensuing decade has seen little by way of progress in this area.[14] Nor is it any surprise that *when actually given a choice* about what she wants for her life—this being the truly radical development here—more and more women are opting to *lean out* of motherhood and redefine what "having it all" means for them.

For any woman without kids, this means giving yourself full permission to pursue your overarching ambitions for your life, in terms of your career, your security, and your overall well-being, without feeling guilty about it or like you will be "missing out" if this does not include motherhood. Think back to the exercise in Chapter 1—what came up as your non-negotiables for living the life you desire? Now consider how many of the things you "want" are things that other people—your parents, society—*want* you to want. Ask yourself: What must you prioritize and what might you have to sacrifice in order to achieve your most heartfelt ambitions for your life? How might (or how does) being a parent impact your ability to pursue these things?

These are the kinds of questions to ask if having it all is to become less about ticking off boxes on a prescribed list of accomplishments, and more about determining *exactly what it is that you need and want* to live a fulfilling life. No more, no less. Needs and wants that we are all equally entitled to regardless of our start in life. Needs that begin with material security. Security that gives us the freedom to choose what we want for our life. Choices that, in turn, are linked to the *desires and capacities* that help determine where a woman may find herself on the Motherhood Spectrum and that are intertwined with adrienne maree brown's orgasmic YES! A yes that is the pilot light igniting the fire in the bellies of the women we were born to be.

* * *

At the time of writing, it is estimated that the childless-by-choice (the Affirmative No's) make up around 10 percent of women without kids—with the majority thought to be childless-by-circumstance: they would like to have kids, but things just haven't worked out. They can't afford it, they haven't met a suitable co-parent, or they've experienced fertility issues. Increasingly, their plans are on hold due to concerns about the environment (what you might call "childless-by-climate-change"). But just as our circumstances can dictate our choices, the choices we make also shape our circumstances going forward. So where does being childless-by-circumstance end, and being childless-by-choice begin?

As I was beginning work on this book, I had a conversation with a friend who found herself questioning her life choices after undergoing treatment for breast cancer in her mid-forties. Having been brought face-to-face with her mortality, was there anything she wished she'd done differently? A successful multidisciplinary artist who has toured the world with rock bands, written multiple books, and scored countless films, it was only now that she was deeply anguished by her own inconvenient truth: that despite always wanting kids, and doing her best to prioritize finding a partner to create a family with, she hadn't managed to make it happen. In her case, she felt that "every choice I ever made that was *not* prioritizing having a kid is the reason I'm not a mom." Walking the streets of New York City's Lower East Side, the hard, blank, midday sun bleaching the graffiti off the sidewalks, there was an urgency in her voice when she told me: "Younger women who are on the fence need to be aware of this." Meaning, it's not enough to assume it will "just happen" while you go about attending to what feel like higher-priority aspects of your life.

Not that plenty of those reading won't be painfully aware of this already.

But what my friend was talking about are the micro-decisions relating to a person's ambitions and aspirations, as well as their overall well-being and quality of life, that may lead her down the path to non-motherhood without her really noticing. The decision, for example, to move to a city with high rents and a competitive job market in order to pursue a certain career path. The choice to stay, even if it means being located far from a wider family network who could potentially help with childcare. Same goes for deciding not to settle for a less-than-ideal partner to co-parent with; allocating part of your budget to a gym membership or regular therapy sessions; pursuing further education; or prioritizing travel, a lease on a car, or eating out with friends over stashing any spare cash away in a baby fund.

Which choices, big and small, have you made for your life that have influenced your reproductive outcomes? Looking back, is there anything you would have done differently? To be clear: there is no shame in prioritizing your career or your personal comfort over becoming a mom. Everything I've listed above is representative of the kind of comfortable, autonomous, middle-class existence that is the bread and butter of the American Dream. Even if, in reality, most of these things remain luxuries that are only available to a privileged few.

. Which feels like as good of a place as any to take a closer look at the "selfish" tag that is often applied to women with-out kids. Especially the childless-by-choice, whose decisions not to procreate are often seen as indicative of an inability or an unwillingness to put the needs and wants of others—in this case *an as-yet-unborn child*—before their own. Sometimes, this man-ifests in overt criticism and judgment of a person's character and life choices; at others, it snakes into the conversation as snarky unconscious bias. In the assumption, for example, that women without kids have tons of excess time on our hands, which we could (and perhaps should) be dedicating to helping raise other people's kids. But isn't it equally self-serving to bring a whole new person into the world just because you believe you will find happiness and fulfillment in parenthood?

When I told another older woman without kids that I was planning to call this book *Selfish Cunt*, she was more offended by the s-word than the c-word. How do you feel about the word "selfish"? What is selfishness, and can this be applied to any of your life choices? How have these choices impacted the other people in your life? In many cases, deciding to channel one's energy and other resources into alternative paths to motherhood simply means being realistic about one's *parental readiness*—a concept I have touched on a couple of times, and which speaks to one's material, mental, and emotional capacity for raising kids. Something, again, that women have only been permitted to even contemplate in the past half-century.

When I knew for sure that I would have an abortion, it wasn't because I am a cold-hearted bitch who was refusing to share the *gift of life*. Rather, I intuitively just knew that I wasn't cut out for motherhood. At the time, I could only vocalize this inner knowing by citing the practical reasons for ending my pregnancy: "I can't afford to have a kid" and "I want to focus on my career" (both of which spoke to a desire to prioritize my material stability). But in the decades since, I have touched base, again and again, with the *feeling tone* of my decision. This process has found me mining the depths of my subconscious, where I have come face-to-face with all the anxieties, the insecurities, and the neuroses that had always made me doubt whether I had what it took mentally and emotionally to be a mom.

A few years ago, one of the glossy magazines I used to work for ran an article titled: "Am I Willing to Risk My Mental Health to Have a Baby?" "I sometimes think that guarding my sanity so ferociously makes me selfish," the writer shared, detailing how a combination of therapy and medication had finally helped her overcome her chronic anxiety and OCD and find some inner stability. But her mental health took a nosedive after she fell unexpectedly pregnant (she miscarried after three weeks). Now age thirty-six, her biological clock tick-tick-tocking, she found herself asking, "Do I want a baby, but my anxiety is masking that desire and convincing me it's a terrible idea? Do I fear what will happen to my brain if I get pregnant again? (Yes, yes, I definitely do.)" Her angst radiated off the page. But actually, how fortunate to be aware of this ahead of time, the better to help orient oneself on the Motherhood Spectrum. Let alone have the option not to become a mom, and to instead invest one's time, money, and energy in one's own emotional and mental well-being.

Not least for the sake of one's potential offspring. It was around the same time that I also learned about something called "childhood emotional neglect" (CEN). This is what happens when, usually through no fault of their own, a person's primary caregivers are unable to properly validate the emotional life of their kids and tend to the unseen, inner needs that must often be coaxed out of hiding. Perhaps this is because the parents experienced CEN themselves, perhaps because they are experiencing mental health issues, or perhaps because they just don't have time to be fully present with their kids. Those who experience CEN can grow up with a pervasive sense of something being missing; that "something" being the emotional literacy to effectively understand and therefore communicate how they are feeling, and thus develop a solid sense of self. This can result in low self-esteem, perfectionism, feelings of alienation, and a high sensitivity to being rejected—which, in turn, may manifest in depression, anxiety, and addiction.[15]

Meanwhile, practicing the opposite of CEN means bestowing on one's kids that rarest of commodities: *emotional privilege*. In The School of Life book *How to Overcome Your Childhood*, the authors explain that a child receives emotional privilege when a parent (among other things) is able to "put their own needs aside for a time in order to focus wholeheartedly on the confusions and fears of their offspring; shield [their children] from the worst of their anxiety and the conflicts of their adult lives; [and] reliably seek to explain, rather than impose, their ideas." Given the material, mental, and emotional challenges of parenthood, the authors also posit that true emotional privilege is "as rare as huge wealth," with those who receive this in childhood deserving "to be counted among the true one percent."

Which is not to gloss over the very real privileges of growing up with money. Children raised in households with financial insecurity are more likely to experience poverty as adults while also being at higher risk of developing chronic conditions such as asthma, obesity, heart disease, and diabetes. Not that this is ever the parents' fault, and not that CEN can't also be present in wealthy households. Meanwhile, more people would be "parentally ready" financially if we saw radical reform of economic policies and working conditions—the wider implications of which we will be exploring elsewhere. For now, when considering *all that you need and want* in order to live a fulfilling life, and the things you may well prioritize as a result, I'll say it again: it is not selfish for these to include choices that are as much about comfort and peace of mind as they are about necessity. To prioritize these things over having kids.

Yes, having a child means making personal sacrifices when it comes to one's freedom, time, energy, and finances—and self-sacrifice is as worthy a quality to cultivate as any. Especially in a rampantly unequal society. But the only kind of society that tells women it is *selfish* to pursue other things over becoming mothers, including safeguarding our own material, mental, and emotional well-being, is a society that oppresses women. Sadly, having the option not to have kids before we are ready—which might mean not having kids at all—remains a privilege in and of itself. One you could say we owe it to future generations to exercise. But when talking about equality, we also have to ask ourselves: what do we actually *need* to thrive, how much is it okay to *want*, and when is enough truly *enough*?

* * *

The truth is, for many of us living in capitalist, consumer cultures, having "enough" ideally means having *more* than enough. More food in our cupboards than we need to eat, more clothes in our closets than we actually wear, and more money in the bank than we need to cover our basic expenses each month. For many people, of course, this is not the case, for whom living on the breadline, check to check, creates a constant background hum of desperation and despair—with financial anxiety being a major factor in suicides in the United States.[16] Money might not buy happiness, but it does create a safety net, which in turn is what allows us to relax and enjoy our life. Viewed through this lens, it is also okay to want "more than enough" and to factor this in to our decisions about parenting.

Given that single motherhood significantly increases a woman's risk of falling into poverty, largely due to the fact that the gender pay gap disproportionately impacts mothers,[17] the fact is it often feels safer to prioritize the controlled rewards of the working world. Meanwhile, the handmaiden of consumerism is a workaholic culture in which the hustle never lets up—and which equally leaves little space for family life.

Personally, I was raised in a home where it felt like there was never quite enough; Mum would even save the vegetable water for soup, and my brother and I shared a bedroom that was divided in two by a plywood partition until I was fifteen. But my father's wealthy parents also paid for me to go to private school from grades six to ten, where my classmates were dropped off in Mercedes and Lamborghinis. Dying from shame, I would make Mum park around the corner in her tomato-red Citroen 2CV. While their parents ran companies and had second homes in France, we spent our vacations in a two-room wooden shack with no running water on the banks of the river in Suffolk. And when things got extra tight, on occasion my mother would even borrow money from me. Growing up "mixed-class" meant I got to see firsthand exactly what money could buy: security, space, and plenty of nice *stuff*. Stuff that made life feel smooth, and warm, and beautiful. When I grew up, I told myself, I would make sure I always had enough to buy the things I wanted. An outlook that seeded the skills I would need to make it in an increasingly competitive world: fierce ambition, an urgent need to succeed, and a perfectionist work ethic. Qualities that I also suspect would make me a miserable mom.

We tend to think of the 1980s—the decade that spawned the infamous phrase *greed is good*—as the apex of consumerism in Western culture. But in my subsequent magazine career, I spent my twenties and early thirties documenting a culture of excess. It was the early 2000s, the era of *Sex and the City*, Brazilian waxes, and the WAGs—the "wives and girlfriends" of British soccer stars who became famous for their ability to bestow $1,500 handbags with *must-have* status. All of which only dialed up the volume on my desire for financial abundance.

And, if anything, the advent of the internet—and social media in particular—means the message that happiness can be bought has only become more insidious, with the credo "I consume, therefore I am" swimming in the collective consciousness like the microplastics in our bloodstreams. The compound effect of all of *this* as it pertains to our procreative choices? The dirty little truth is that amassing *more than enough stuff* has subliminally been positioned as a faster, cleaner, and less complicated source of happiness and fulfillment than having kids.

When I consider what I might have to give up in order to become a parent, I am pretty disappointed with myself. Working less hours while simultaneously having to support another human being means there would be no more $8 lattes on my coffee breaks, no more regular massages, no nice hotels on trips back to the UK. I know my privilege is showing here—and it feels super exposing. This is also where I get ripped to shreds on social media (which is ironic, given that Instagram and its ilk are the worst culprits when it comes to presenting lavish lifestyles as the ideal normal). But few men are ever questioned for prioritizing their paycheck, or shamed for how they choose to spend it. And I'm also not alone here, am I? What are the less-than-essential things you might have to "sacrifice" in order to become a mother, and how do you picture your life without these things? If this brings up any feelings of shame, or even self-disgust, what do you think makes you want the things you do?

Reflecting on all of this, the title of a 2021 *Vogue* piece caught my attention: "I Deeply Love My Kid, I Just Can't Stand Playing with Him." In it, the author describes coming up with new ways *not* to play with her child, her favorite being to buy him things instead (and so bestowing on her son the emotional inheritance that consuming is soothing). "Music class at the local library, play-dates, playgrounds, parks, and pretend still make me want to do almost anything else, still make my brain feel numb and bored and uninspired," she wrote, her words recalling the intense restlessness that I too experience whenever I am around young children and their aimless games. But can you blame us? In a culture where time is money, and where money—and not necessarily family, as we have seen—is what brings security, happiness, and fulfillment, "play" feels boring because it is a waste of time.

Which is all just more information to help you orient yourself on the Motherhood Spectrum. If, like me, you're somebody who claims to love their career, and who has made this your primary focus, how much of this is because you love the work itself—and how much of it is because of what it gives you, in terms of financial security and the trappings of a more comfortable life? Again, there is absolutely nothing wrong with prioritizing the latter. Even if, in an ideal world, enough time, money, and other resources would be readily available to all, without us having to hustle like our lives depend on it.

For now, the fact is that having kids can seem like a prohibi-tively costly endeavor, especially when weighed against what we might have to give up. That sometimes, in a consumer culture, *stuff can even feel better than love*. Which I realize makes me sound like one of those ball-breaking 1980s career women. Also: *selfish cunt*. But seeking a sense of security and fulfillment in work and consumerism does not make us stupid, amoral, or selfish; in a consumer culture, it's like we're wired to want *more*.

The other irony is that the more affluent a society, the more financial freedom women have, and the higher our status in society, the lower the birth rate overall. There's a chicken-and-egg scenario at play here. On the one hand, women become better off when they are not channeling their resources (time, energy, and money) into raising kids. And on the other, increased access to higher education, travel, personal development, and creative pursuits, as available to women in wealthier nations, expands our life choices exponentially. Pursuits that are all "wants" as opposed to "needs" (and that could also be classified as "stuff")—but which, unlike $1,500 handbags, have enabled women to dream of *self-actualization*.

The gilded cherry atop Abraham Maslow's Hierarchy of Needs, self-actualization, speaks to the drive to fulfill one's highest potential—usually through the realization of one's natural gifts and talents. This need is innate to all human beings, and it is part of what makes life feel meaningful. What would self-actualization look like for you? Being free to explore whatever this might mean for me was what my parents were getting at when they told me they just wanted me to be *happy* when I grew up. With this as my goal, I've been incredibly lucky—and have worked incredibly hard—to be able to make a living from my writing. Something else I might have to "give up" if I became a mom, in favor of a job that comes with healthcare and a more regular paycheck. And yes, there have been times when I've leaned on S and the stability of his corporate career. But these roles were reversed when the competitive toxicity of the corporate world led to him experiencing suicidal ideation in his mid-forties, and he decided to quit and take a time-out to work on his mental health. A story for a whole other book, and a resignation, and a period of necessary inner-excavation, that would not have been an option for him had he been supporting a wife and kids.

After all, under capitalism, a person reaching their "highest potential" often looks less like following one's calling, and more like pursuing whatever career path comes with the biggest salary and benefits package attached. No matter what they may have to sacrifice in terms of their mental health and personal fulfillment in the process. For women, meanwhile, self-actualization has long been linked to having kids—inherent in the notion that motherhood is what "completes" her. Even while, as one subject laments in *Regretting Motherhood*, "In the first days after giving birth, I realized that, from then on, it was expected that I, a person with pains, feelings, desires, and aspirations, would set myself aside for an unlimited period of time, diminishing myself, disappearing, becoming obliterated."

It was also always a myth that self-actualization is the result of "having it all"—even if pursuing self-actualization *does* require one to have enough. This is because each layer in Maslow's "pyramid" of needs can only be attained once those below it have been met. Beginning with the basics (air, food, water, sleep), we then graduate to safety needs: financial security, a place to live, employment, and physical health. Next come our needs for belonging, intimacy, and connection. After this, our "esteem" needs: respect, status, recognition, and personal freedom. And only once we have attained all the safety, belonging, freedom, and respect that we need are we free to turn our attention to our highest vision for what we desire for our life. As things currently stand, this is what makes self-actualization *as we know it* a function of privilege: safety, belonging, freedom, and respect, often linked to our earning capacity. And therefore easier for women to access when we don't have kids.

So, if self-actualization is the goal, how do we create a world where everybody gets to have everything they need and want to live a comfortable, happy, and satisfying life? A life where all beings get to live freely as themselves—including the as-yet-unborn children circling this juncture in our story like fireflies in the ethers, waiting for their moment to join in with the evolutionary scrum we call *humanity*. In a consumer culture, being "comfortable" is literally synonymous with being "rich." But what about a world where comfort is the norm?

This would actually be a world in which Maslow's hierarchical pyramid is dismantled altogether—the structure of which mimics that of Eisler and Fry's top-down domination systems—and in which security, belonging, freedom, and respect are instead spread evenly throughout the population like double-chocolate vegan frosting. As it stands, unless we're working proactively for equality for all beings, then the climb *up the pyramid* essentially means stepping on all those still struggling to get their basic needs met: that is, the low-wage workers (often mothers) and third-world laborers (often children) whose energetic output is sucked up and externalized as the hidden human cost of production.

In and of itself, not having kids is not going to create the conditions for a more equitable world. This will ultimately require a shift to a values system that emphasizes caring and interdependence. But within this, *women not being expected to prioritize motherhood above all else* is also a prerequisite. Why? Riane Eisler's research has shown that "[in societies where] the status of women rises, in both the family and the state . . . men [also] start to embrace more stereotypically soft, caring policies." What she means is that as women gain more influence, "power" is no longer associated with typically "masculine" traits of competition and dominance. Instead, we see that collective empowerment lies in collaboration. And the fact of the matter is that more women gaining more status, and therefore having more say in how the world works, will require more of us to continue to have fewer kids. It might not be immediately obvious in terms of how you live your daily life, but the simple fact of you unapologetically claiming the mantle of woman without kids makes you a part of this shift.

Not that moms can't, or don't, wield enormous influence in business, politics, and the culture at large. But we can't all be Wikipedia women. There is simply not enough time, energy, and other resources for the majority of women to have an impact outside of the home in addition to raising kids. Currently, the only women who are able to do this are those who have the resources to *do it all*—the education, the childcare, the finances, the community support, the energy, and the self-esteem. Women who are also more likely to have been the beneficiaries of unearned privilege—including, perhaps, emotional privilege—somewhere down the line. It is no coincidence that three of the most progressive figures in US politics today—Kamala Harris, Stacey Abrams, and Alexandria Ocasio-Cortez—are all women without biological children of their own. Would these powerful women, who all come from backgrounds that have historically been oppressed, have had the opportunity to "lean in" to their legacies had they also been raising children of their own?

Ultimately, every woman without kids who proudly walks this path (whether she chose it, or it chose her) is helping to make it okay for women not to have it all—perhaps to not even *want* it all. To figure out what is "enough" for them. She is staking a claim for all women's self-sovereignty and bodily autonomy. And she is doing her part to help overturn the outdated and extractive myth that self-actualization is more about boxes ticked than it is about us becoming the people we were born to be. This is a powerful part of what unites our unsung sisterhood. Ultimately, as demographer Amanda Jean Stevenson notes: "Maybe there are fewer babies right now, but people are able to live the lives they want to, and that's a profound thing." Profound, unprecedented, deeply feminist—and as revolutionary as it gets.

"

"I don't see my friends that have kids very often. Interestingly enough, none of my close female friends have kids. We're all in our mid-thirties. It's honestly kind of nice. We go on trips together, see each other often, have stayed close."

— **age thirty-four, newly married**

"I want to talk about getting divorced when you have no children. I was married for ten years, and when I got divorced, I felt like people just thought, 'Oh well, they'll just move on. No real attachments.' So wrong. While I didn't have children to have to worry about, I still had myself. It was just as hard. In fact, I sometimes wonder if having kids doesn't make it more likely that you'll develop a good relationship with your ex. You have to figure out a way to communicate."

— **age seventy-three, divorced**

"I thought that dykes got a total pass on this mother stuff. Now there's a pressure for queers to have kids, too?"

— **age fifty-one, married**

"

CHAPTER 6

Found Family

FEBRUARY 29, THE YEAR 2000: it was now or never. S and I were on a night out with our housemates, walking the short, dark distance from the bar to the entrance of Fabric nightclub in Smithfield's Market. Today was supposed to be the day, and now it was getting late. Fuck. I grabbed his hand: "Hey, I think we should get married," I blurted out. It had taken two vodka tonics and a pint of Stella for me to muster the courage to say out loud what had been circling my brain for the past two weeks. But now I wasn't sure he'd even heard me. My words made frosty little clouds in the nighttime chill, where they mingled with the faint reverb of the bass line emanating from the club. When I'd practiced in my head, it had sounded far more romantic: "I've never felt this way before; *will you please, please* marry me?" Fuck! Had I fucked it up? But then we were pushing inside, as the bass filled our ears with sound until there was no more space for words.

It had been almost a year since our first kiss, and little over six months since I'd moved my stuff into his scruffy, ivy-clad share house in South London. When we'd discussed me moving in, we'd been clear that if it didn't work out, it would not mean we'd have to break up. But so far, all good. S ran a music public relations start-up with his mate out of an office in an ex-council block in Brixton, and Dylan, the "dad" of the house, was one of his DJ clients. Then there was Roo, who grew up with Dylan on a commune in Suffolk; shaggy Dave; his Kiwi girlfriend, Maura; and Dylan's ex's sister (who we couldn't work out if he was having a thing with or not). A French intern at the PR firm was also currently crashing in the tiny box-room, her stuff stacked at one end of the single mattress that took up the entire floor space. Which officially brought our number to eight (eleven, if you included the cats).

Having grown up in a family like mine, where people talked *about* each other as opposed to with each other, being welcomed into this ragtag household felt like walking onto the set of *The Waltons: The Psychedelic Edition*. Spats over the washing-up roster played out against a backdrop of constant banter and music industry chat. There was also access to a steady drip of alcohol: blood-red bottles of cheap merlot lined up like bowling pins on the kitchen counter and shots of citron-flavored Absolut straight from the freezer. Sometimes Dylan would bring his decks into the living room and the house would fill with cigarette smoke and party people who would stay for days. And at the center of it all, him.

The notion that S and I should *make it official*, however, had snuck up on me out of nowhere, after I realized that the turn of the new millennium would be ushered in by a leap year. February 29 being the once-in-every-four-years window when a woman was "allowed to" propose to her man. The concept was so quaintly sexist, wouldn't it be ironic if I went ahead and did it? Especially given that marriage had never even been on the agenda for me. Being a wife was nowhere near my list of aspirations. But now this. *Now him.* "I can't imagine ever not *liking* him," I told a friend I'd confided in about the proposal I could feel percolating. Not that this accurately described what I felt when I was with him, which was closer to a profound sense of *relief* that I had found someone it felt completely safe to be myself with.

Back at Fabric, our gang had taken over a corner table in the upstairs VIP room. S did the PR for the place, and he had a platinum-colored card imprinted with the club logo that manifested limitless free drinks. A balcony overlooked a sea of bodies on the state-of-the-art bodysonic dance floor below, where underfloor speakers vibrated the music up through the soles of your feet. A tropical mist of cigarette smoke, sweat, Impulse body spray, and dry ice hung over the crowd, the whole place pulsing to the heartbeat rhythm of the bass. Then I felt S come up behind me and place his hands on my hips. *Now. Do it now!* When there was a break in the DJ's mix, I turned to face him, pulling him closer so I could shout into his ear: "Will you then? Will you marry me?" The bass dropped back in at that exact moment to an ecstatic whoop from the crowd, obliterating his reply. But the next thing I knew, he was kissing me, and we were being passed around the housemates in a continuous, looping group hug. I heard Dylan's voice booming out above the horns and hoots that filled the air: "Fuck yeah, you're getting married! Somebody get the fucking champagne!"

As far as proposals went, it was kind of a mess. It turns out neither of us actually wanted a *wedding*, either. The whole thing seemed like such a performance, and we both cringed at the thought of reciting our vows in front of relatives we barely knew. It would be another three years before we got up the courage to elope and officially tie the knot. Which meant I was twenty-seven years old when I became Mrs. Warrington, taking his name being part of the whole "ironically unfeminist" package.

I was also the first among my friend group to get married, and almost immediately people wanted to know: "So, when are you going to *start a family?*" Meaning, *when are you going to have kids?* The fact we were married but did *not* plan on having children made us both the most traditional and the most unconventional couple around. People just couldn't get their heads around this: I could see their brains short-circuiting as they tried to process the fact that it would always be *just us*. In the heteronormative order of things, it was like not having kids—or even wanting, trying, and failing to have kids—would mean not fully consummating our marriage. And the fact that "starting a family" is synonymous with having children is inherent to the notion that you will never have a *real family* of your own until you become a parent.

So, how *do* you make a family when making babies is not on the agenda? This question is central to the experience of women without kids, for whom the concept of Found Family—that is, the ones besides our blood relatives who just feel like *home*—is front and center in our lives. Regardless of a person's relationship status or their connection to their family of origin, not having children of one's own can create what feels like a kin-shaped hole in a person's life. So let's take a closer look at why this is, along with the ways in which we can begin to close the kinship gap.

* * *

The reason we associate "family" with "children" in the first place is because the classic nuclear family consisting of two (heterosexual) parents and their offspring is still very much considered to be the *ideal-normal*[18] and therefore the only legitimate kind of family. Not least, as Adrienne Rich explains in *Of Woman Born*, because within this construct, "the man assures himself of the possession of his children; through control of his children he insures the disposition of his patrimony [or material inheritance]." There are also undoubtedly benefits to this setup: when a man knows his children are *his children* he's more likely to want to help look after them.

Not that this is guaranteed. On the not-so-plus side, humans also tend to have a pretty hard time with monogamy, and when all one's eggs have been placed in one tightly woven basket, the end of the marriage essentially means the end of the family. But it's like the blood that inked this ancient contract has left an indelible stain on our collective psyche: we just can't stop trying to make it work—to the extent that the ideal-normal of the monogamous nuclear family has even been adopted among queer communities, with the advent of same-sex marriage being seen as a win for LGBTQIA+ rights.

But the truth is that many people born from the late 1970s onward did not benefit from the supposed order and stability of the classic nuclear family setup. Our baby-boomer parents were the first to reject the stuffy traditions of their families of origin *en masse*, the emergence of the teenager in 1950s pop culture recognizing for the first time that young people had a right to minds and lives of their own. I've shown you some of how this manifested in my family system. What is the nature of your parents' relationships with their families of origin? And how has this influenced your connection to your biological family system? As boomers—my own parents included—pushed back against the restrictions of the traditional nuclear family, rates of separation shot up in the 1980s after no-fault divorce gained legal traction. As a result, many of us were firsthand witnesses to our parents' often acrimonious breakups, and some have also had to navigate the complex emotional terrain of our parents' remarrying and starting whole new families that do not include us.

Growing up against this backdrop, how could we not experience a degree of cognitive dissonance when it comes to reconciling the *marriage-and-kids* mandate with our lived experience of family life? As one character in Sheila Heti's *Motherhood* puts it: "The fact that they broke up the family, means we didn't feel obliged to carry it on." Have your feelings about having kids been influenced by being raised in a "broken" home? Meanwhile, if we are the product of a family system in which the women and children have experienced oppression and abuse (even if this predates our arrival on the scene), then having the option not to repeat this cycle can be both freeing and empowering.

Queer activists in the 1980s are credited with having formalized the concept of Found Family—also known as "chosen family" or "family of choice." Having experienced prejudice from their biological families due to their sexuality, a person's Found Family became a refuge, a home base, a community, and a support system all in one. In an ideal world, community and mutual support are what families are for—and anybody who feels alienated from their family of origin will be familiar with the process of recruiting unrelated individuals to be *our people*. Meanwhile, the fact that more and more of us can relate to the concept of Found Family is also part and parcel of an unstoppable demographic shift: the decimation of human tribes and of traditional extended families. A development that is alternately framed as both the tragedy of our times and part of our evolution on the path to greater individual freedom and flourishing.

In a 2020 *Atlantic* magazine cover story charting this unfolding and its impact on the overall social structure, conservative columnist David Brooks unpacks "the story of the family, once a dense cluster of many siblings and extended kin, fragmenting into ever smaller and more fragile forms"—and concludes, "Today's crisis of connection flows from the impoverishment of family life." Said crisis having manifested in what some have even termed a *loneliness epidemic*. For example, one-person households have increased from 118 million worldwide in 1980 to 334 million in 2020, coinciding with a spike in rates of addiction, depression, and suicide, and widening economic inequality.[19]

All of which Brooks claims are products, in part, "of a family structure that is too fragile, and a society that is too detached, disconnected, and distrustful." A sad indictment of the times.

But having kids brings no guarantee of family: it is estimated that one in four US adults is estranged from their parents.[20] Galit Atlas believes this figure is an undercount, since "others have stopped short of completely cutting off contact but have effectively severed the ties."

Meanwhile, when it comes to coupling up with a suitable co-parent, having no partner is infinitely preferable to having a partner who routinely abuses, undermines, or disrespects you, or who you just no longer want to be with. Remaining nobody's mom may also be a more realistic and appealing prospect than struggling to make ends meet as a single parent. And while more people remaining single for longer is often framed as them being "too picky," it is actually a reflection of people's increased autonomy over their lives. Women's especially. As noted, it is only in the past thirty to forty years that we have gotten more familiar with the concept of family dysfunction, as well as what constitutes mental and emotional abuse.

In *Beyond Motherhood*, Jeanne Safer notes that among the women she interviewed for her book, there was little evidence to suggest that a higher percentage of women without kids came from dysfunctional family backgrounds—save, perhaps, for them having "a slightly higher than average percentage of unhappily married mothers or frustrated parents." Well, she was writing in 1996—most of her subjects having come of age *before* divorce rates began to rise in the 1980s. Among my friends without kids today, many come from family backgrounds that would be considered less than ideal: they are the daughters of divorce, they are estranged from their parents and/or siblings, or they've had to fight rigid cultural rules about how they are expected to live their lives. In short, much of what Safer's subjects' mothers were conditioned to accept as "functional" and "normal" in terms of family life and intimate relationships might now be recognized as anything but.

Can you blame us for holding out for something better, even if this means forgoing parenthood *in this lifetime* and focusing on our Found Family connections instead? If anything, perhaps it is time to remake the notion of "family" entirely, and to focus our energies on creating Found Family systems that validate, nurture, and support the people we were born to be. Found Family systems that may well not require us to have children of our own—and that women without kids are poised to help pioneer.

It's a mindset shift that has been decades in the making. Back in 1986, researchers in the Netherlands were studying a global phenomenon that came to be termed the Second Demographic Transition (SDT).[21] It was predicted that social and economic developments from the 1970s onward would bring about sustained sub-replacement fertility (less than 2.1 children per woman), a multitude of living arrangements other than marriage, a disconnection between marriage and procreation, and continuous mass migration. All of which, my friends, has come to pass. Meanwhile, the SDT is also associated with individualism, with more opportunities for *self-realization* being given as one reason for the lower birthrate. This same individualism has enabled freer, more autonomous, and (supposedly) more affluent lives, and it has driven much immigration to places like the United States—the fabled *land of the free*. And nothing is more freeing than having no dependents.

Carried to its logical conclusion, it could be said that individualism is at the heart of our crisis of connection. It can make us less willing to compromise or sacrifice on privacy and personal comfort when it comes to our living arrangements, for example, hence the rise in single-person households. And on a more macro level, when the drive for personal advancement goes unchecked, it can create a culture of competitive, me-against-the-world self-seeking.

But then, differentiating ourselves as whole human beings with needs, wants, and desires for our lives that are unique to us and that may not be aligned with the values of the dominant status quo—including our family of origin—has equally been a necessary part of dismantling the domination systems that have ruled the past few centuries. Domination systems that have imposed rigid ideas about home and family life and continue to stigmatize queer people, single people, and non-parents. The fact is, the marriage-and-kids mandate that has so long been considered the bedrock of family life no longer reflects the needs and values of the societies we live in and the individuals we are still very much discovering ourselves to be. In contrast, our Found Family systems should do exactly that.

* * *

They say it takes a village to raise a child. From the practical to the emotional to literally everything in between, mothers need the support of other mothers almost as much as their children need them. But the truth is, we all need a village, all the time, no matter our familial or marital status. Said "village" provides all the conditions that sociologists have identified as being necessary for forming close relationships: proximity; repeated, unplanned interactions; and a setting that encourages people to let their guard down and confide in each other. For some, our village will be a bustling hive of activity with weekly townhalls, and for others it will be more of a one-horse town with a monthly mail delivery. Either configuration is perfectly okay, so long as it serves you. And while they are increasingly hard to come by in our individualistic world, these villages tend to constellate at the places where we come together in our shared interests and needs: at college, at work, among volunteer groups, and in recovery circles, for example.

Also in motherhood, where birthing a child *supposedly* grants immediate access to a clucking, bosomy coven united by the shared experiences of birthing and raising children. From the outside it can seem like this is the case; non-motherhood sometimes leaves one with the sensation of gazing through fogged-up windows at a holiday feast we did not receive an invite to. I know you've felt this too. But in reality, many of my mom friends report feeling equally alienated from other mothers—especially when their parenting style fails to conform to expectations. In some cases, they tell me, admittance to the *mom cult* can even feel like it requires the erasure of the person they were before they had a kid; in the eyes of society and the other moms who now make up their default extended family, they are seen first and foremost as the mother of their child.

But still, there exists an aura of solidarity among mothers. When one friend became pregnant (it turned out to be a phantom pregnancy that she would go on to "miscarry") she immediately got calls from her mom friends welcoming her to the club. Meanwhile, for women without kids there is no equivalent sisterhood. No specific "thing" to bond us besides the empty space that society dictates should be filled by our offspring. Which means we have to get proactive about creating this sense community and sisterhood for ourselves. I wrote this book in part because I feel the need for this in my bones; I hope that you are here because you feel it too. So, how to go about creating this in our lives? And what differentiates Found Family from our regular friendships?

When it comes to the "how" of creating Found Family, I picture an interdependent network of people who have got each other's backs, no matter what, and who are able to let each other know what we need, when we need it. When it comes to the "who," I like to say you'll know them when you feel them. Words that come up for me when I think of how I would like family to feel are attentiveness, acceptance, and trust. The people I count among my chosen kinship group are the ones it feels safe to be myself with, the ones who check in on me without me having to ask, and who I get a sense won't judge me, no matter what.

Who reflect back to me in a way that goes beyond words that I am valued, appreciated, and essentially an *okay person*. Who are the people in your life that come to mind as you are reading this? What are the shared experiences that have helped to create these connections? And what would it look like on your part to prioritize and double down on your commitment to these relationships?

In my case, thanks to a combo-platter of introversion, trust issues, and hyper-self-sufficiency (many of the same personality traits that place me at the Affirmative No end of the Motherhood Spectrum), finding these people has been few and far between. Part of the reason S and I shied away from a traditional wedding is that we were embarrassed by how few people we would want to invite. Weren't weddings a celebration of all the loving connections you had made throughout your life? And didn't *not* having an abundance of these to show make you sort of a *sad case*? But "more" most definitely does not equate to "better" when it comes to relationships, especially in the context of Found Family. And then some, for more introverted types. In fact, according to British anthropologist Robin Dunbar, known for his research into human relationships, "[Introverts] prefer to have fewer friends so they can invest more time in each. Extroverts are more socially confident, so they prefer to have more friends at the expense of investing less time in each. . . . These are just two equally good ways of solving the same problem."

The "problem" in question being that human beings *need to need each other*—the extent to which we feel we "need" somebody in our life being perhaps the true differentiator between friendship and Found Family. Needing each other, and being there for others when they need us, is the yarn of healthy interdependence that knits our human family together. From the moment we arrive on this earthly plane, we need other humans for everything from food, shelter, and employment, to information, belly laughs, and hugs. Have you noticed how, in addition to being there for others, your connection deepens even more when you ask somebody to be there for you?

Something that gets in the way of this is that our hyper-individualistic world has groomed us to meet our own needs first and foremost. Needing each other is the very *social technology* that is under attack from the apps that have become our first port of call for access to much of the above. Most apps are designed to make life more convenient, with many of the services they offer—from podcast conversations to meal delivery services, to text therapy—catering to the needs of the lone individuals who make up our *post-family world*. But the more convenient life is, the more self-sufficient we become. And the more connected we are online, the less we need to interact with others IRL: the more *inconvenienced* we feel by the time and effort it takes to maintain our flesh-and-blood connections, and the less inclined we are to reach out in the first place. In the 2021 documentary *The Wisdom of Trauma*, Gabor Maté goes so far as to observe, "What we call civilization demands the denial of human needs." And when we no longer need to need one another, the question is whether or not we need families at all.

In many ways, the emergence of app culture has been a core accellerator of our crisis of connection and the resulting loneliness epidemic. Nowhere is this more evident than in the realm of romance. Journalist Julia Bainbridge hosts *The Lonely Hour* podcast, which aims to destigmatize the loneliness that so many modern city dwellers in particular experience in their daily lives. Another woman without kids, she talks about the "video-gamification" of dating, with apps such as Tinder having amped up the point-scoring nature of the activity. This in turn creates a transactional environment that makes it harder than ever to make and maintain intimate relationships. Yes, the kinds of relationships that might lead to one *starting a family*.

Among those who've grown up on social media, this has manifested in another interesting outcome: a 2022 poll showed that 58 percent of millennials and seven out of ten Gen Z adults would rather adopt a pet than become parents, it being far less complex to form loving bonds with furry "family members" than with other human beings.[22] In addition, people who have experienced childhood emotional neglect often form strong attachments to their companion animals as a reliable source of "unconditional love."[23]

In a way, social media could be seen as a necessary stand-in for our village, the place we go to find *our people*. But if anything, amassing more and more "friends" on Facebook, Instagram, TikTok, and the rest creates a mirage of connection—while squeezing the time and energy we have available for the actual human beings in our lives. And though it can be a great place to find like-minded individuals . . . the flipside can be less tolerance for individuals who *don't* think just like us (if the algorithm even lets us know that they exist). In flattening the nuance of human interactions, social media makes us faster to judge and quicker to write people off—when what creates lasting bonds is our capacity to repair any ruptures with others using our uniquely human skills of empathy and acceptance. Skills that algorithms are not programmed with, and which we must actively practice with one another.

We can do this through storytelling; through deep listening; through proactively checking in with one another IRL; and with our willingness to let other people be exactly who they are, versus who we want them to be, the latter being the natural consequence of greater self-acceptance. For any woman without kids who is invested in growing our sisterhood, honing these skills is not optional—it is essential to creating the kinds of Found Family networks that are vital to our thriving and our well-being.

* * *

Above all, needing and being needed by others, as well as feeling understood and knowing that we'll be forgiven for our mistakes, is what lets us know that we *belong*; a sense of belonging is perhaps the greatest human need of all and another big, important function of family. And in some ways, becoming a mother automatically fulfills a need to belong: a woman will always belong to her child, who will always belong to her. Even if becoming a mother finds many women struggling with their new identity, the sense of belonging to another human being *no matter what* holds a potent and alluring promise in a culture of constant churn that can make us all feel somewhat disposable. But instead of pining for the family we don't have and staking our belonging on human beings who do not yet exist, what would it look like to put more of our time and energy into building a village from the relationships we've already got?

Studies have shown that it takes between forty and sixty hours of togetherness to move from an acquaintance to a casual friendship, eighty to a hundred hours to call someone a friend, and over two hundred hours for someone to be rated as a "best friend."[24] Meanwhile, if a friendship lasts longer than seven years, psychologists say it will last a lifetime. Seven years, in the scheme of things, is not that long. But still, it pales in comparison with the time we spend forging connections with our *family* family without even thinking about it. In the first year of our infant life, we will likely spend over eight thousand hours in close proximity to our primary caregiver and other immediate family members, whom we have no option but to entrust with meeting our material and emotional needs in their entirety. Whom we have no option but to trust, period, regardless of whether or not this trust is earned.

The interactions we experience with our primary caregivers during the first five years of our life (so, the first forty thousand hours or so) also wire our entire nervous system and have a profound impact on our capacity to form relationships in later life. Regardless of the quality of the care we received, or how these relationships play out, biologically speaking it's no wonder we feel a profound and often inexplicable sense of loyalty to these people. This also gives some insights into the level of sheer togetherness that is required to form "familial" connections with people who are not part of our biological clan. Two hundred hours is roughly one full week (or 1.5 weeks if you factor in time for sleeping). But as adults, how often do we give anybody a full week of our uninterrupted, emotionally open and vulnerable companionship?

In terms of the practicalities of forming Found Families, another *Atlantic* article painted a progressive picture of what this might look like when it asked: *What if Friendship, Not Marriage, Was at the Center of Life?* The article profiled individuals whose most significant others fell somewhere between being spouses, siblings, and soulmates: "They live in houses purchased together, raise each-others' children, use joint credit cards, and hold medical and legal powers of attorney for each other. These friendships have many of the trappings of romantic relationships, minus the sex." And yet, with no clear category for them (participants use terms like "platonic life partner," "my person," or "Big Friendship"), they are often not taken as seriously as official spousal partnerships. Is there anybody in your life who you have this kind of connection with, and who you could imagine making a life with if so? What would be the value to society of friendships like these being legally recognized, as with gay marriage?

These are the friendships that bring to mind historian Richard Godbeer's observation that "we can love without lusting," but friendships like these take time, energy, and conscious effort to maintain. Based on your experiences, what is needed from us as individuals to create and nurture our Found Family ties? And when do these bonds tend to become frayed? Keeping the friendship/Found Family fires burning can become even more challenging when one of you has kids. Each time a close friend has announced her pregnancy, I have felt an immediate surge of joy, my heart simultaneously breaking at what this likely means for our relationship. The same way friendships are impacted by other major changes and life events, such as one of you moving to a different country, getting a new job, or quitting drinking, for example, changes in our schedules, needs, and priorities mean it will likely never be the same between us. A woman's child will always need her in ways I never could, and her becoming a mom will introduce her to experiences and emotional challenges that I will never be able to empathize with.

This can be extra painful in the early years, when it can be hard for the non-mom friend not to feel as disposable as one of the baby's diapers; the sheer intensity of the bond the new mom is forming with her child also shines a light on the transient nature of mere *friendship*, and how quickly ties that may have endured decades can dissolve like cotton candy in the rain.

Not that I haven't also been the one doing the dropping; in both of my long-term romantic relationships I've hunkered down into isolated togetherness with my partner. The first time because his assumed ownership of me was total; the second because it was just too easy, too cozy, and too comfortable to not want to be together all the time. One friend who is single without kids describes this retreat into domesticity as "pulling up the drawbridge." "Just because you have a traditional family unit [now] doesn't mean you should cut off ties with your chosen family and friends," she lamented, of what can feel like cold-blooded acts of betrayal. How have your close female friendships been impacted by marriage, cohabitation, and motherhood? And what cultural conventions have played a part in this?

Not that any ruptures therein are usually intentional. What's needed in these situations is an acknowledgment of how changing circumstances will impact the friendship, and a willingness to adapt and compromise on both sides. This is arguably easier when you're *not* the one holding the baby and managing a sleep deficit the size of China while contemplating the overnight demolition of your life as you know it. But it is equally important for moms to let their non-mom friends know that we still matter to them. These negotiations are both practical and emotional in nature, and they take time, effort, and a willingness not to take every unanswered text or lapsed catch-up call personally. There also needs to be acceptance that things likely *won't* ever be the same, but that this doesn't mean that all the hours invested in the friendship have been for nothing, and that it can't evolve into something else.

It's also natural, given that cohabitation is the easiest way to guarantee the conditions that facilitate deep connection—*proximity, repeated, unplanned interactions with others, and a setting where (ideally) it's safe to let it all hang out*—that the people we call family are the ones with whom we make our home. For the majority of adults, this means a long-term partner or spouse, and any kids that have sprouted along the way. But so much is lost within this siloed way of living, which places undue pressure on a person's partner or children to be their *everything*. This setup, along with the rise in single-person households, also does nothing to support our broader human need for interdependence. Too often, as Orna Donath writes in *Regretting Motherhood*, "The [nuclear and/or biological] family ends up as a veritable sponge, sopping up any loving concern which might reach the world outside. . . . Babies and children, especially our own, can make us lose sight of the community as a whole." The odds might be stacked against us, but in light of our *crisis of connection*, this is just another reason to prioritize our Found Family ties—parents and non-parents alike—as well as the effort and consistent nurturing it takes to maintain them.

* * *

But can Found Family ever *really* be a substitute for biological family? Traversing a newly digitized landscape while tending to the wounding that so many of us have sustained as a result of the decimation of community life, plenty of people are invested in figuring this out for themselves. Often, this does involve new ways of thinking about *home*; from polyamorous intentional communities, to co-being collectives for global nomads, to experiments in intergenerational living, hopeful humans everywhere are seeking ways to build Found Families that meet the needs of all involved—whether or not they have kids. Profiled in *The New Yorker*, one of the founding members of genderqueer "intentional family" the Rêve, a commune-type complex in upstate New York, explains, "The thing that I wanted was a family. And I didn't want to get married or have children. And it turns out you can still have a family, even if you're not getting married and having children." In fact, creating *Found Family* systems might even be easier when you don't have kids.

Elsewhere, the Israeli Tarbut Movement is a nationwide collective made up of roughly three hundred core members engaged in a communal lifestyle. Some live in commune-like groups, and others have formed co-living complexes that offer a greater degree of individual autonomy. All decisions pertaining to "family life" are made by consensus, and, crucially, groups within the movement also share their finances. I learned about Tarbut from a younger woman-without-kids friend, whose brother has been a member for the past seven years. Observing his involvement with the movement, "I have come to see 'family' simply as an interdependent network of support," she told me. Something she is applying to her own thinking about if, when, and with whom she wants to "start a family" beyond her existing biological clan.

Meanwhile, it was only in 2014 that the first Tarbut kids began to be born, and interestingly, this development has posed the greatest threat to the movement's longevity, since "dealing with the normal and daily routines of [childrearing] brings the members closer to the normative structures they wish to defy," she noted. In other words, it is becoming biological parents that brings members face-to-face with the social conditioning and emotional inheritance of their families of origin—often creating a schism between the progressive values of the movement and more traditional notions of what a family should be.

For the majority of people, meanwhile, the idea of cohabiting with groups of other adults, let alone sharing finances with nonblood relatives, remains pretty radical (twenty-three years into our union, S and I have never shared a bank account). Does anything about these ideas appeal to you? What do you think you would find most challenging about enacting them, and why? The closest I ever came to experiencing something like this was the three years I spent in Dylan's South London "commune," where our bonds were mainly formed along narcotic lines. But I also haven't seen or heard from any of the housemates for years, and at the time of writing, hope for the future of family life feels thin on the ground.

Navigating the social wasteland that emerged in the fallout from the COVID-19 pandemic, the compound effect of days, weeks, and months of social distancing had brought two essential truths into laser focus for me: that without consistent nurturance, the closest of friendships can quickly wither and die; and that when the chips are down, *family* family still often trumps Found Family. Besides S, the people I spoke to most during the pandemic were my mother and my brother. Not the ones that I have chosen to be my family, but the ones that this life chose for me. Scrolling the contacts on my phone, I found myself questioning what had felt like the surest of friendship bonds. Was the fact nobody was calling me because of something I'd done, or simply a consequence of all the times I had neglected to call them? Once it became possible to actually plan some visits, I hesitated: who did I even want to see? And who would have space in their new post-pandemic lives for me?

Of course, there was also the fact that none of us *needed each other* like my mother needed me, quarantining by herself at age seventy-three. When I began calling her each Sunday, it was the most regular contact we'd had since I was fifteen. Curled on our sofa, night after night, my cozy intimacy with S had also led to new levels of isolated coupledom during the darkest days of the outbreak. But with the sirens wailing outside our windows, and death literally on our doorstep, it had also become impossible to ignore the stark reality of our situation: if he died first (all the odds suggesting that he would be the one to die first) then one day it would just be me. This is a vision that haunts many a woman without kids, especially given how many well-meaning individuals think it is helpful to ask: *but who will look after you when you're old?*

It's not like I wasn't fully aware of my predicament already. Whenever the realization had surfaced in the past, I'd applied an intellectual Band-Aid to the problem in the form of abstract, sci-fi ideas about installing walking, talking holograms of the people I cared about to keep me company in my dotage. There being robots to bring me my meals. The hope that by the time I am unable to keep myself clean, laws will have been passed allowing me to end my own life painlessly and with dignity at the precise time of my choosing. But this time, it led to me experiencing the closest I have come to a physical urge to be a mom. At age forty-five, I finally got it: having a kid would mean making more of *us*. It would mean literally making a whole, human person, who would be ours no matter what. *Like a raging hunger, but in the heart space*: what I felt, glued to my phone and wondering where my people had gone, was a primal *yearning* for family. A surge of pure emotion that was powerful enough to momentarily override how unsuited for parenthood I know myself to be.

But wanting family is not the same as wanting to be a mom. In my case, the sensation dispersed in cascading waves of sadness.

Sadness for the grandparents I had never hugged, and for the aunts, uncles, and cousins who felt like strangers to me. Sadness for my parents, and their disconnection from their families of origin. Sadness for the abuse, financial hardship, mental illness, and festering resentments that prevent families everywhere from loving one another unconditionally. Sadness for the ways that modern life has atrophied our capacities for patience, understanding, and intimacy. And for all the ways in which the family structures that nurture our humanity have been manipulated by domination systems that offer the promise of security in exchange for unquestioning conformity.

In sobriety circles, there's a lot of talk about the "void." The unnamable blank space on the inside that we seek to fill with food, and drugs, and love, and work, and all the other *stuff*. That sometimes feels so dark, and so deep, that it could swallow us up. Allowing myself to fully feel all of the above was like staring directly into this abyss, a hole in our society that is icy cold and dark as midnight. It made me realize that, for many of us, the void *is* the space where a supportive, loving, and interdependent family network used to be. All of which has made me wonder: how many people become parents simply in an attempt to fill this hole? If we continue to value ease and convenience over mutual interdependence, how can it not keep getting deeper and wider? And how can we get better at turning toward *each other* to soothe our cravings for connection, instead of passing this collective family dysfunction on to the generations to come? This is what our Found Families are for—but they will only be as strong as our willingness to invest in them, something that I have tried to make a priority in the wake of the pandemic.

In my other lonely old lady fantasy, me and my non-mom friends have somehow swung it so that we all live together on some kind of a compound or other. We each have our own private space, we take turns to cook, and we pool our resources to pay for whatever additional care we may need. We have created our own village, basically. The logistics of actually creating this feel unrealistic, but if anything, my post-pandemic realizations have left me feeling more inspired than ever to focus on the kinds of Found Family connections that I hope will ripen and mature as I age. As did a conversation with Jody Day, whose Gateway Gatherings initiative seeks to create local, intergenerational connections between women without kids. "A lot of the support we need as we age is not intimate care. It's somebody to pick up our groceries, or drive us to the doctor," she explained. "As I move into my sixties, I am mentoring women who are in their forties. This way, when I am in my eighties, I will have a pool of younger women around me to help out." The "local" piece being key to the success of Day's vision.

What she's describing sounds to me like the very essence of sisterhood, doesn't it? How do you envision your interpersonal relationships playing out as you grow older? And what actions can you take in your life today to create the kinds of connections that will stand the test of time? If I can leave us with anything here, I hope it's the sense that when approached with vulnerability and intention, and when we don't take for granted that it will "just happen," it is always possible to find the kinship that we need. That within this, every woman without kids can fulfill the need to be needed and find her place to belong.

"My grandmother lived through the depression and told me frequently that it was essential I be able to 'take care of myself.' Given that challenge, taking care of others (i.e., kids) seemed beyond my capacity."

— age sixty-five, single

"I am half Filipina, and in the Philippines children are automatically considered blessings. People also take care of each other there. Growing up in the US, where families get very little support and have to fend for themselves, I got different ideas. Rather than blessings, I see children as burdens."

— age thirty-seven, married

"The thoughts of raising a brown child in this racist, white culturally dominant society are absolutely fear inducing."

— age forty-five, single

CHAPTER 7

A Duty of Care

CARING FOR MY HALF-BROTHER, who I will call Joseph here, is a four-person job. It takes his parents, my father and step-mother, for starters: one to manage the meds, the meals, the *admin*, and the other stationed by his side, around the clock, to monitor for seizures. Sometimes there will be more than fifty small "drops" in a day, each one delivering a jolt of adrenaline to the solar plexus of all in the vicinity. What you don't want is for it to progress to a full-blown *tonic-clonic*—or grand mal seizure. I have only witnessed this a handful of times, his lanky, young man's body going stiff as a board, eyes rolling skyward, breath caught in stasis, as his face and lips turn a cornflower shade of blue. Not knowing which way to look, as his parents fly into action: "JOSEPH. Come on, love, *come BACK.*" And then, *gulp*, "*there* he is, you're okay, it's okay." The panic subsiding as his eyes come back into focus, self-conscious, frightened, and confused. If he doesn't snap out of it then, it will mean a trip to the ER and potentially several days in a medically induced coma to prevent further seizures.

And then there are the in-home caregivers. A roster of empa-thetic, stoic young men who come by in pairs to sit and read or

149

color with Joseph, or take him for a walk, buying his steadily aging parents the time to shop, and bathe, and breathe, and pee. Dad was filling me in with the latest developments in their daily routine during one of the rushed biannual lunch dates that had come to form the basis of our relationship since I'd moved to the United States. He was seventy at the time. Making his way through a plate of breaded chicken tenders, he spoke in a matter-of-fact monotone. I picked the onions out of my salad as I quietly absorbed the slow, gloomy flow of information, noticing with a stab of concern the tiny tremor in his hand as he lifted a forkful of food. *Was that new?* The doctors, he continued, still didn't have any answers, just the ever-mutating cocktail of meds that may or may not, over the years, have stunted Joseph's cognitive growth. Might have actually made his condition *worse.* They had been trying to wean him off the most deadening of them, but it was a delicate process. Cut the dose too fast, and the seizures would come on like a rash. "But, you know, it's best that he's back home," Dad concluded.

When Joseph had turned eighteen—a legal adult—he'd become eligible for a place in a full-time residential care facility. A move that meant his parents would also get some respite. But the care just hadn't been up to scratch. They'd visit to find him in food-stained clothes, stuck in a wheelchair in front of the TV. What were they feeding him? Was he getting *any* exercise? The final straw came after a big seizure took him down while he was there, out of sight but never out of mind, and with nobody to catch his fall the impact took out a tooth. Now he wore a helmet at all times.

I was twenty when Joseph was born, fully submerged in the ghostly twilight zone of my relationship with Adam at the time. A last-minute addition to the family, the signs that something was *not quite right* with Joseph were there from infancy, the fuller picture revealing itself as the years ticked by. There were the seizures, sometimes mild, sometimes terrifying. There was the autism diagnosis, which explained the lack of speech. There were the special schools, the special doctors, and the special combinations of drugs. There were the endless reams of paperwork that unlocked government funding for his care.

When I'd visit, I'd hover in the margins, unsure of how to interact with him. I'd grasp his hand and give it a squeeze, ducking my face to try to make eye contact, the recognition of our sibling bond registering momentarily. But as I became caught up in the busy hustle of my magazine career, I'd watched from a cautious distance as his parents' world became gradually smaller, more insular, and more focused on the specifics of their child's needs. When Joseph was younger, his mother still went to her office manager job three days a week, and Dad squeezed a few lectures in here and there. But since the care facility hadn't worked out, and with the seizures having gotten steadily worse as the years progressed, either of them leaving the house for longer than a few hours at a time had become something of a *mission*. And now here they were: locked in an intricate performance of caregiving that was so all-consuming, so specialized, and so intuitive that nobody could possibly replicate it.

But they also won't be around forever, and as his next of kin, one day the responsibility of caring for Joseph will fall to me. Won't it? It's a conversation that's been hard to have. To take over where they leave off would require me to abandon my life as I know it; my husband too. The notion seems otherworldly, but with severely limited options in play I have pictured it often.

After all, here I am, a fully functioning, spare adult with no dependents of my own: it seems only logical that I should step in and fill the caregiving gap as needed. In reality, this will likely be when he moves back into full-time residential care. Maybe you already have other ideas about what I "should" do. And I'm curious: what would *you* do? However things play out, the shape of our shared fate looms large, like a hurricane gathering momentum on the horizon before making landfall in my life.

I haven't ever acknowledged Joseph in my writing before, mainly because I can't get his permission. But I also can't not include his part in my story here. There could be no starker an example of the sacrifices parents make for their kids, and of the lifelong and unpredictable nature of the vocation. Having a child like Joseph also adds a whole new dimension to the concept of parental readiness. Not that he is not beloved, and not that parents of disabled people everywhere aren't able to find extraordinary meaning and fulfillment in the role. For my part, having Joseph be part of our family has broadened my perspective on the human condition beyond measure. What I have witnessed with my own eyes about the reality of raising him has made one thing very clear: *that when you have dependents, you need others you can depend on.* Something, as discussed, that is anathema to the slick self-sufficiency that is both the goal and the lonely outcome of our culture of individualism.

As we have also seen, for many women without kids, the truth is that the more self-sufficient you are required to be, the less time, energy, and other resources you will have at your disposal to channel into motherhood. Because the majority of your time, energy, and other resources must be channeled into caring for *you*.

Of course having others you can depend on is supposed to be what families are for; all the more reason to get serious about nurturing our Found Families if for whatever reason we are separated or estranged from our families of origin. But what Joseph's situation also illustrates is that families need structural support that goes beyond the home. His is an extreme case, but all parents rely on a wider network of care to meet their and their children's needs. At a minimum, this extends to professional childcare, schooling, and healthcare services—the COVID-19 childcare crisis having shined a light on just how fragile these vital structural support systems often are. The sum of all of this means that anybody with dependents is at a disadvantage. Another factor that is having a profound influence on the lives and the choices of women without kids.

* * *

As if those struggling to make ends meet as single parents, who rely on free childcare from grandparents (as is the case for 40 percent of families in the United Kingdom and the United States),[25] or who are faced with footing the bill for their parents' eldercare aren't painfully aware of this. Don't live in constant awareness of the paper-thin line between staying afloat and struggling for air. As if residents of cities with ballooning unhoused populations aren't confronted with the daily, devastating reminder that one lost job, one lapsed rent check, or one mental health break, *and it could be you.*

At the same time, dwindling natural resources are being spread increasingly thin and uneven, the wealth of the world accumulating in fat, opaque globules of empty luxury real estate in New York, London, and Silicon Valley. As the rich get richer, and the poor get poorer, the stakes for survival only get higher. This leads to a situation where, as philosopher and futurist Jaron Lanier puts it, "The economy only works now if you are young, healthy, and childless."[26] Or a wealthy, white conservative.

In the United States, it is conservative Republicans who have the biggest families: that is, those whose interests are most aligned with the ideals of heteropatriarchy. In the 2020 US election, the incumbent President Trump did considerably better in counties with higher birth rates.[27] And yes, this suggests that the conservative right will continue to gain traction as each new generation reaches voting age (assuming that their offspring inherit their parents' political views). That's why they call it *survival-of-the-fittest*—conservative values constituting "fitness" in a society that rewards conservatism. In his *Atlantic* article on the death of the extended family, David Brooks also notes that "affluent conservatives often pat themselves on the back for having stable nuclear families . . . but then they ignore one of the main reasons their families are stable: They can afford to purchase the support that extended family used to provide—and that people further down the income scale cannot."

By this he means the "babysitting, professional childcare, tutoring, coaching, therapy, [and] expensive after-school pro-grams" that are often what set a person up to thrive (let alone survive) in a hyper-competitive "meritocracy." As well as affording parents the time and space to care for their own needs so that they can be fully present for their kids. Essentially, the wealthiest members of society get to buy themselves a village. Without these supports in place, as trauma expert Clementine Morrigan notes, "It is almost impossible for people to 'properly' parent their kids. Let alone heal their own intergenerational trauma."[28]

As we have seen, while the right not to have children is a hard-won privilege for womankind, being able to afford to have kids has become something of a privilege in itself. This paradox is exacerbated for women of color, as found lurking beneath the testimonies of the young Black and brown women profiled in a *New York Times* report on an increase in the number of people delaying motherhood. "I can't get pregnant, I can't get pregnant," Luz Portillo, the oldest daughter of Mexican immigrants, tells her-self in the piece. "I have to have a career and a job. If I don't, it's like everything my parents did goes in vain." Meaning, becoming a mom will make it that much harder for her to fulfill her family's dreams of her achieving financial prosperity.

Building on what came up for you in Chapter 5, what kinds of structural supports would you need to have in place for your own material, mental, and emotional security not to be compromised in parenthood? To what extent has a lack of access to these supports influenced your feelings about becoming a mom?

For a woman like Portillo, exercising the privilege of non-motherhood is an empowering choice (regardless of whether she decides to have kids later on). It also makes her part of what feminist scholar Jenny Brown frames as a twenty-first-century "birth strike" in her 2019 book of the same title, in which she charts an in-depth history of women's unpaid childrearing labor. The way she frames it, "Women in the United States are staging a production slowdown, a baby boycott, in response to bad conditions. Determining that the burdens are unfairly piled on us as women, we're deciding to have fewer children or none at all."

But in some ways, this helps to reinforce the message that motherhood is a woman's natural role, the implication being that if free childcare, extensive paid parental leave, and universal healthcare, for example, were made readily available to all, then we would happily open up our cunts and resume business as usual. This makes Brown's argument less relevant to the Affirmative Nos. But the ultimate aim of her book is to help individuals stop blaming themselves for not being able to balance their desire to have a comfortable, happy life with a desire to have kids. In an interview, she told me that when many women decide they can't afford to have children, "We think, 'I shouldn't have got into so much student debt, I should get a better paid job, or find a cheaper apartment.'" But this frames an inability to "do it all" as a personal failing, when the truth is that parenting is an unpaid, full-time job. One that, without proper supports in place, very few people are able to take on without it impacting their financial stability overall. What's more, Brown wants to make it clear that "the system requires our unpaid childrearing labor in order to function. It's designed that way. Once we can see this, we can also see that it could be designed another way."

Her solution? If the goal is to make it possible for people to have the families that they want without having to sacrifice their basic well-being, this means putting policies in place to ensure that mothers and their children receive the support they need. But not pronatalist policies, such as offering cash bonuses to new parents or criminalizing abortion, which simply emphasize having more kids without taking the overall well-being of families into account. What's needed are *pro-family* policies, which encompass everything from paid parental leave, to free universal healthcare and childcare, to higher wages for shorter work weeks, to higher salaries across the spectrum of the caregiving professions—from teaching, to nursing, to food production, to maintenance work.

Pro-family policies could also be said to extend to environmental policies that address the basic human right to exist as part of a regenerative and biodiverse natural world—an area that can no longer be overlooked in conversations like these. And they must also include free and easy access to birth control and abortion (Brown was a key figure in the campaign to make the morning-after pill available without a prescription). Because a truly pro-family society would also make it okay for women *not* to have kids, if, for whatever reason, we do not feel financially, mentally, or emotionally ready for them. If there are other things that we feel we have to contribute, and other dreams we want to pursue. And, not least, if we do not have other people in our life who we know we will be able to depend on once we have children who depend on us.

And yes, in my case, I have a husband I can depend on. But in addition to him having faced his own mental health challenges, it had always seemed obvious to me that many of the things that are integral to the success of our marriage—long, uninterrupted conversations; lavish amounts of personal freedom; a quiet, tidy house; and some savings in the bank—would be seriously compromised by bringing a child into the mix. The breakdown of my own parents' marriage and the dysfunction of my family history has also left me with doubts as to the "unconditional" nature of both familial and marital bonds. My parents having separated

when I was so young, and having experienced firsthand the instability of being raised in a de facto single-parent household, how
could I be sure it wouldn't go the same way with us?

Given the current lack of state provisions for our other most
vulnerable populations—the disabled, the elderly, and the
sick—it is a given that many of us will also be responsible to
some degree for our aging parents' care. Especially those of us
whose families were scattered like autumn leaves by the divorce
boom of the 1980s and 1990s. Having an aging single mom who
relies on her children for support—and not because she messed
up, but because things like careers, and mortgages, and pensions
were not readily available to women of her generation—is a relatively new phenomenon. Is this something you can relate to?
It's a situation that represents another rumble of thunder on the
horizon in the lives of many women without kids: *If I must care
for her, then who will care for me?* Meanwhile, nobody asks men
who don't have children, "But who'll look after you when you're
old?" It is assumed that having been a "provider" his whole life,
he will look after himself.

This conundrum would be allayed in places like the United States
by the implementation of universal healthcare, for starters, as well as
better work opportunities and lifestyle solutions for older people. And
besides, having a kid to ensure there is somebody there for us down
the line requires an investment *now* that many cannot afford—and
that also comes with no guarantees. For every dutiful daughter making
monthly payments toward their mothers' eldercare, there are parents
dipping into their pensions to help support their adult children and
their kids. When I posted about this subject on social media meanwhile,
one comment said it all: "I teach in an assisted living facility and can
attest that not all kids visit their parents in the nursing home." Again,
my father's case is an extreme example of how the opposite can equally
be true: he remains his son's full-time caregiver in his seventies—which
also renders him unavailable for grandparental duties.

Generations of women having grown up in single-parent households has left another legacy too. When we spoke, Jenny Brown
shared that she and her colleagues had also engaged in raising
consciousness around their own decisions regarding parenthood.
This meant having conversations that took them time-traveling
back into their own experiences of being mothered. Like me, "A
lot of us had seen our mothers struggle. Parenting looked exhaust-
ing and difficult, like no fun at all. Of course, [our mothers']
hard work was supposedly for our benefit, but we realized that if
we then threw ourselves into it for the sake of our own children,
nobody would ever just get to enjoy their life."

And so, the dominos continue to fall; for as long as our societies do not prioritize the support that families need, then those of
us who have the option will continue to have fewer kids.

* * *

Simply put, an instinct not to pursue motherhood often reflects an
awareness of just how hard it is to be a mom. That as it stands, the
joy and the gifts of parenthood are too often stifled by the struggle. But the truth of the truth, the real kick in the womb, is that
it shouldn't be. If motherhood is something she is drawn to, then
becoming a parent *should be* one of the most joyful and fulfilling
experiences of a person's life. Equally, being mothered *should be* the
foundation of a secure sense of self and what teaches us to trust that
the world is essentially a safe place.

Undoubtedly, policy changes and ideological shifts incorporating those mentioned above would improve the lives and
outcomes for caregivers and more vulnerable people across the
board. Would make it easier for those who are on the fence
about having kids to either pursue parenthood with confidence

or to feel more secure in their choice not to. But what is not so often invoked in conversations like these is the potential damage done *to the kids* by our lapsed societal "duty of care." That is, our collective responsibility for creating conditions that minimize the potential for harm to the general population. Ultimately, it is children who suffer the most when their caregivers are not adequately supported in the role of raising them.

For example, children who experience inconsistent caregiving (and possibly CEN) due to a parent or caregiver working long hours outside of the home—whether for minimum wage *or* as a requirement of a high-pressure corporate role—are more likely to experience attachment issues. This in turn will make a person more susceptible to depression, anxiety, and addiction, and it will also make it harder for them to form secure adult relationships themselves in later life.[29] The kind of relationships which, in an ideal world, form the foundations of healthy family systems.

In a 2015 TED talk, California surgeon general Nadine Burke Harris spelled out how more extreme cases of childhood trauma and neglect affect health outcomes across a lifetime: "Exposure [to trauma] dramatically increases the risk of seven out of ten of the leading causes of death in the United States. In high doses, it affects brain development, the immune system, hormonal systems, and even the way our DNA is read and transcribed. Folks who are exposed in very high doses have triple the long-term risk of heart disease and lung cancer and a twenty-year difference in life expectancy."

The kinds of "trauma" she's talking about are outlined in the seminal Adverse Childhood Experiences (ACEs) study, and they range from physical and emotional abuse, to neglect, to losing a parent due to divorce or incarceration, to domestic violence, to having a parent with a mental illness, to addiction in the home. It is also worth noting (especially in light of Amy Coney Barrett's 2021 suggestion that "safe-haven" laws permitting women to drop unwanted babies off at fire stations are a viable alternative to legal abortion[30]) that 50 percent of the unhoused population and 80 percent of people in prison spent time in foster care while growing up.[31] Adverse experiences such as these are exacerbated by the social and economic stressors placed on parents by structural inequalities, and they could be mitigated by these being directly addressed. But then, instances of child abuse and neglect are also prevalent in the most "privileged" of homes. In an ideal world, a duty of care would therefore also include a radical new approach to how we think about mental and emotional well-being.

In short, lack of proper support for families across the board has created something of an intergenerational pileup when it comes to the health and well-being of society overall—as evidenced by a rise this millennium in what are termed "deaths of despair" (from suicides, drug overdoses, and alcoholism).[32] Often attributed to the erosion of both family life and working-class prosperity, this can also be framed as the toxic emotional inheritance of centuries of heteropatriarchal oppression and extractive capitalism. The true impact of which has only begun to become apparent in the past few decades—coinciding again with the steep drop-off in the birth rate.

The original ACEs study was published in 1998, and it has only been since the early 2010s that the subject of childhood trauma has infiltrated the wider mainstream consciousness, with an explosion of books on the subject being published in the past decade. And it's a subject that millions of people outside of the medical profession are hungry for—*because many of us have lived it*. For example, the 2014 book *The Body Keeps the Score* by trauma specialist Bessel van der Kolk has been published in thirty-six languages. As of July 2021 it had spent more than 141 weeks on the *New York Times* nonfiction bestseller list, with twenty-seven of those weeks in the number-one position.[33]

Given the links between childhood trauma and adverse health outcomes, van der Kolk even goes so far as to claim that in the

United States this is "our nation's largest public health problem." One that also creates billions of dollars of wealth for health insurance companies and Big Pharma. One way to tackle this problem would be to *better support mothers in their mothering*. For anybody in any doubt about their material, mental, and emotional capacity for parenthood, another might be to prevent these issues from presenting in the first place *by not having kids*. In what ways, if any, were your own parents compromised in their capacity to care for you, and why? How has this impacted you, both as a child and as an adult? Taking into account the notion that *hurt people hurt people*, how might you prioritizing healing your own childhood wounding benefit the other people in your life?

Improving outcomes for the families of the future is the mission of human rights lawyer Carter Dillard's Fair Start Movement, which aims to change the laws, policy, and culture that inform our current procreative ethics. For Dillard and his "Collective" (which, he was keen to emphasize when we spoke, is made up primarily of women and people of color) this means shifting the focus from what potential parents *want* (to fulfill a fundamental human need for belonging) to what future children *need* (family systems that are properly supported in nurturing and caring for them).

"Every child deserves a fair start in life," Dillard told me, spelling out the three pillars that are the foundation of his work: parental readiness, birth equity (canceling child tax credits for high earners, for example, and using the money to create bonds that poorer kids themselves can access later in life), and encouraging people to have smaller families. For many, this means delaying parenthood for as long as possible; for some, this will mean having no kids at all.

But persuading people to have fewer kids, or forgoing parenthood entirely oneself, is just one piece in a much larger puzzle when it comes to giving parents and their children a better chance at a more comfortable life. For example, reducing the size of the global population is also something of a clarion call for environmentalists. But (as we will see elsewhere) this is only a *response* to the real issue and not necessarily a *solution* at all. If any-thing, this approach continues to make individuals and families responsible for our social, economic, and environmental crises—when it is the extractive domination systems that dictate the shape and structure of our lives that have fucked up both society and our planet beyond all recognition.

Systems, yes, that are made up of the billions of humans that have no option but to operate within them daily. I hate what a hypocrite it makes me to have to be a *selfish cunt* sometimes in order to feel safe and secure. Meanwhile, corporate greed becomes personal greed when an instinct for self-preservation morphs into a culture of unchecked self-gratification. Not having kids isn't going to do anything for society or the planet if the rest of your life is an orgy of competitive overconsumption.

Meanwhile, more people would absolutely be more "paren-tally ready" if wealth were more equally distributed—through fairer taxes, higher wages (especially for blue-collar jobs), and more state spending on quality public services. In fact, just 5.3 percent of the wealth controlled by the four hundred richest Americans could lift every single person in America above the poverty line (around 38 million people).[34] Instead of your taxes being used to fund wars on faraway shores ("men's work," and therefore worthy of economic investment) imagine if they were funneled into state-of-the-art community centers,[35] free college education—which I was the lucky recipient of in the United Kingdom in the 1990s—and universal healthcare that also included unlimited therapy from birth ("women's work" and still devalued in the marketplace). Policies like these would have an enormous impact on the well-being of parents and children alike—*on society as a whole*. They also represent the collective investment that is required now in order to ensure that there are enough new people to care for the steadily aging population.

But the full potential of people being properly supported in their parenting goes far deeper. The emerging field of epigenetics shows that we inherit our ancestors' genetic stress responses, which "switch on" in challenging situations. Tests on how this happens are conducted by traumatizing mice to see how this influences their gene expression. What's interesting about this in the context of our duty of care is the *way* in which they traumatize the mice—which is to either separate them from their mothers or to first traumatize their mothers.[36] Traumatizing mothers, and separating them from their young, being exactly what individualist, survival-of-the-fittest economics does. What if, by taking specific steps to *un*-traumatize mothers and families, we had the potential *to switch off inherited stress responses?* The compound effect would be the population overall starting to orient toward *an innate sense of safety.*

When people feel safe, they are more likely to share their resources and less likely to be goaded into competing with one another for whatever scraps have been made available. The former is essential for a shift toward what Riane Eisler calls a "caring economy"—that is, one that recognizes the enormous economic value of caring, as measured by Eisler's Social Wealth Index.[37] The thinking is that the better care people receive, the better workers do, and the better the economy performs overall. A caring economy also is inherently feminist, antiracist, environmentalist, and pro-family.

Why? Because policies that benefit the well-being of all humans *by definition* benefit all women, all people of color, all indigenous communities, and all kids. People who, at best, are often left out of current economic and social policy—and who, at worst, are persecuted, enslaved, and oppressed. Ultimately, enacting our duty of care to future generations lies in seeing all families—and all people—as intrinsically interconnected and equally worthy of care. It means seeing all of our children as all of our children, regardless of whether or not we have kids.

* * *

This includes those whose needs exceed "the norm." At the time of writing, my brother Joseph is twenty-five years old. If anything, his situation has only become more intractable, as the most recent round of testing has shown his condition to be the result of a rare genetic malformation that a 2019 report found in only thirty-two individuals worldwide.[38] As well as the seizures, his symptoms place him at the most severe end of the autism spectrum. But Autism Spectrum Disorder (ASD) as a whole is thought to affect roughly 2 percent of the population, a number that has shot up threefold since 2000. This increase is attributed to greater awareness, higher rates of testing, better documentation, and changes in diagnostics.[39]

When Joseph was younger, and before he received his official diagnosis, my father would muse quietly on the fact that ASD is also considered to be 80 percent heritable; had the autistic gene been hiding out in the alcoves of our family tree all along? Perhaps that would explain his mother's mental health challenges and his own social awkwardness and uber-intellectualism. On my part, I took this information and hid it deep inside, where I turned it over like a rudimentary tool recovered from an archeological dig. *My acute need for solitude and my discomfort in group settings; my love of research and my obsessive-compulsive routines.* Perhaps some of the same traits that placed me at the Affirmative No end of the Motherhood Spectrum were also signs that I fell somewhere on the autism spectrum. And if this was the case, would I pass the autistic gene on to my child if I *did* have a kid?

Not that I ever shared these thoughts with anybody; me claiming any kind of "disability" feels disrespectful to say the least. Given that I'd had an inkling since age five that motherhood was not for me, it is also impossible for me to parse the extent to which this line of thought has influenced me being a woman without kids. When I had my abortion, Joseph was too young, his symptoms not yet presenting fully, for it to have been a factor. But further down the line, after S and I tipsily conjured baby Sydney, our own imaginary last-minute kid, the possibility loomed like a glowing red stop sign as soon as the initial excitement had worn off. *If in doubt, don't.* Not that there's anything wrong with being autistic, and not that plenty of people don't find an incredible sense of meaning and purpose in caring for a disabled child. But the way in which a person's ASD presents has huge implications for the extent to which their parents' lives will be impacted. Not to mention the level of social prejudice one's child may experience from society at large.

I recently had to explain to my dad what "ableism" is. Despite being Joseph's father, and not to mention one of the only sep-tuagenarians I know who's on Instagram, he hadn't come across the term, which has become something of a social justice buzzword—referring to the casual and often overlooked dis-crimination experienced by individuals with disabilities and/or people who are perceived to be disabled, including those living with conditions such as autism, ADHD, OCD, and dyslexia. Does anybody in your family or wider community have disabil-ities? If so, what has this shown you about our attitudes toward disabled people in general? If not, what is your perception of people with disabilities, and how do you imagine it being for their parents to care for them? Perhaps you identify as being neurodivergent yourself. If so, what specific challenges do you think you would face as a parent—and how might social and structural changes help to mitigate these challenges?

When you start to look for it, ableism is everywhere. Including, some would say, in the prenatal testing that has seen conditions such as Down syndrome being practically eradicated in some parts of the world. For example, in 2004 Denmark was among the first nations to offer prenatal Down syndrome screening to every pregnant woman. Today, nearly all expecting Danish mothers take the test, with 95 percent opting to abort if it comes back positive.[40] This opens up a morally fraught debate about *who gets to live*. The stakes of which have been raised with recent advances in prenatal testing for autism, with commentators fearing that this opens the doorway to "a dystopian future with a distinct eugenics twist."[41]

But this is ultimately about an individual assessment on the part of the person whose life will be most affected—that is, the potential mother—of her capacity to parent a child with disabilities. A parenting role that requires an uber-specific personality and skill set. Being realistic about this is not the same as cosigning a fascist pact to create a master race. But an unwillingness to acknowledge that people with "special" needs have always been a part of "normal" society does speak to our collective *fear of contagion*—a concept I learned about in another of Jeanne Safer's books, titled *The Normal One: Life with a Difficult or Damaged Sibling*.

Fear of contagion speaks to a primal instinct to protect oneself from becoming "sick." We all experience fear of contagion to some degree (and not just while in the grips of a global pandemic), and it is recognized as a core driver of ableism. In her book, Safer also presents it as one of a collection of traits that she believes color the lives of all "normal ones" (her lightly ableist term for the siblings of kids with disabilities), which also includes premature maturity, survivor guilt, and a compulsion to achieve. All of which I can personally relate to, and which I also see playing out in the wider society. Because we all just want to be "normal," don't we? When life boils down to survival of the fittest, any *ab*normalities become a sign of weakness and are therefore to be avoided at all costs.

As such, I see fear of contagion in competitive after-school programs, Instagram filters, productivity hacks, and the billion-dollar #wellness industry, where an almost fanatical focus on "up-leveling" one's individual performance is presented as integral to living a successful life. All of these are examples of what feminist scholar Angela McRobbie calls "resilience training": a safeguard against being discarded or left behind by a society that prizes performance and productivity above all.[42] Partly because this is what capitalism demands of us in order to keep the whole machine ticking along. And on a deeper level, because we fear there will be no safety net to catch us when we fall. In what ways do you engage with McRobbie's "resilience training"? What would happen if you let things slide or found yourself unable to "keep up" with the standards that society has set for "success"?

In a sexist, racist, homophobic, and fat-phobic society, fear of contagion equally extends to the repudiation of anybody deemed "other" than the white, male, heterosexual, cis-gendered *ideal-normal*. Including poor families and single mothers; after all, in a society that makes no allowance for vulnerability, neediness, and personal weakness, having dependents when you have limited resources and/or no one else to depend on is *its own kind of disability*.

The really sick part? This fear of contagion is also *necessary* for maintaining the status quo. After all, privilege only exists in the context of those less privileged; the aspirational ideal-normal in relation to perceived abnormalities or deficiencies. Domination systems need "losers," basically, in order for there to be "winners." To some extent, it is a fear of falling through the cracks, and of ending up "like them," that motivates us to keep working harder and climbing higher, all while creating billions more dollars to line the pockets of the owning class. And all of this because our current economic model is predicated on continual financial growth, and *not* on investing any surplus cash generated on things that people *actually* need to support their physical, mental, emotional, and spiritual well-being.

Survival-of-the-fittest thinking might say that this is the logical, even "natural," endgame of the human struggle for dominance as a species. But a shift to something more like Riane Eisler's caring economy is absolutely aligned with the drivers of our humanity. As Rebecca Solnit points out in her 2018 book, *Hope in the Dark*, "Most of us would say, if asked, that we live in a capitalist society, but vast amounts of how we live our everyday lives—our interactions with and commitments to family lives, friendships, avocations, membership in social, spiritual and political organizations—are in essence noncapitalist or even anticapitalist, made up of things we do for free, out of love and on principle." Things we may have less time for when the majority of our time and energy is being channeled into raising kids.

Solnit's observation speaks to what psychologist Steven Pinker terms our "better angel" human capacities for empathy, mutuality, caring, and nonviolence.[43] Capacities that the authors of *Nurturing Our Humanity* point out "actually manifest themselves across cultures; occur far more frequently than physical violence in any society; *are critical for the raising of the young* [emphasis mine]; and have clear survival value."

Enacting this vision, again, will require us to radically reimagine how wealth and other resources are created and distributed. Beginning, perhaps, and continuing the theme of the previous chapter, with how we think about family. For example, when it comes to legally recognized long-term commitments, philosopher Elizabeth Brake argues that these should be formed on the basis of caregiving—"absolutely crucial to our human survival"—rather than assumed (procreative) sexual activity. This would extend to "friendships, adult care networks, polyamorous groups, or urban tribes."[44] In Joseph's case, his caregivers are more like siblings to him than my other brother and I; they are part of his Found Family. Does it really matter that they are paid to be there for him?

Meanwhile, Jenny Brown believes we need to deemphasize individual achievement and see each human success story as being part of a group effort. In my case, this means me acknowledging

Joseph's helpers as being part of a network of care that also allows me to do what I do. As Brown notes, while we celebrate prize-winning scientists, novelists, and athletes, "what about the person who held their hand on their first day of school, or taught them to read, or helped to produce the food they eat." Ultimately, "seeing ourselves as more interrelated would [also] make it easier to see the value of investing in children and parenting." Would make it easier to see the benefits of this for all beings, as well as for the future of the planet.

As for the specific role of women without kids in all of this? We'll be looking at this in more depth in a bit. But being realistic about one's parental readiness, and not bringing a child into the world if you have any doubts about your capacity to care for them, is a great place to start. I repeat: it is not selfish to put your own security and well-being first. But it also definitely means being more conscious of how we choose to invest any economic and social capital that is not being funneled into raising kids: where we spend our money, how we spend our time, and the ways we leverage our individual skills and networks to help contribute to greater security and well-being for all.

For anybody who is feeling the void of disconnection in our post-family world, regardless of our reproductive identity, it may also mean filling the spaces where we feel the lack of family the most with projects and causes that directly address our crisis of connection. For all of us, this means being there for one another in whatever ways we can. It means asking for help when we need it, and allowing others to be there for us. And it means *slowing down* with the uber-productivity for long enough to cook each other meals, hear each other's woes, and give each other hugs.

But perhaps most of all it means noticing how we treat those whose needs exceed the norm, or who appear "different" or less able than us. The roots of our fear of contagion run deep, like weeds sucking the nutrients from the soil of our togetherness.

Left unchecked, the belief that some people are inherently more valuable to society than others *is* ultimately what fuels fascist domination systems. But when we can acknowledge, accept, and commit to our duty of care for the most vulnerable, needy members of society, we are also better able to acknowledge, accept, and care for these parts of ourselves. This is how we will each be restored to our full humanity; this is how our individual healing can help to heal the world.

"

"I saw how broken my mother was, and I didn't agree with her assertion that her personal sacrifice should be seen as a gift/blessing to me. That rationale didn't make sense. I didn't want that 'gift.' It creates an unwanted expectation that I should meet her needs. I would have preferred for her to find fulfillment through personal exploration and growth."

— age forty-one, single

"As a teenager, there was a long period of time when I felt like I genuinely hated my mother. That must have been so difficult for her to experience; I never want anyone to make me feel the way I likely made her feel."

— age thirty-one, married

"I feel sadness over not having children, not guilt. But I do not regret my choice, because for me, choosing not to get pregnant has been in the best interest of the hypothetical child. A child deserves a healthy and loving home, with mentally healthy parents. I have not found myself in a relationship that I feel can provide this."

— age forty, married

"

CHAPTER 8

Home
Truths

AT THE VERY START of our journey together, I asked us to
consider the emotional inheritance of our origin stories and how
sometimes not having kids means something is ending with us.
Elsewhere in this text, we've examined the evolution of sexual norms
and the breakdown of traditional notions of family, along with the
impact of the social and economic fallout from these phenomena
on people's procreative potential. Within this, the revolutionary rise
of women without kids can be read as part intuitive adaptation,
part conscious course correction, and as a sign that we are ready to
rewrite the script going forward. But while it's one thing to focus
on boldly forging a new narrative for womankind, there comes a
point where there is no more avoiding our personal and collective
home truths: those gnarly, barbed unspeakables that we must *accept*
as part of our stories, as part of *us*, if we want to be free of their
underhanded influence as we move forward.

I have touched on ways to approach this process wherever I have
asked us to begin to unpack the centuries of conditioning that are
behind so much familial and societal dysfunction. A process that began
in earnest for me after I moved to New York City, and which kicked

into high gear at age thirty-seven—which is how old I was when my mother began a conversation with me that would change our relationship forever, as well as become a vital component of me making my peace with being a woman without kids.

She had been visiting S and me in New York City, her things neatly piled next to the sofa where she'd been camped out like a nesting sparrow in the middle of our one-bedroom apartment. The October air outside was apple crisp, the fall colors filling the windowpanes with shifting shades of gold and green. But as usual, we'd run out of things to talk about by day two, the curtain of awkward quiet that often hung between us as dense and as heavy as a Dickensian London smog.

She hated me being on my laptop when we were together, often chided me for putting work before family, but that afternoon the lure of escape into my inbox had been too strong. Without thinking, I'd gravitated to my little desk, where I quickly became so absorbed in the stream of digital distraction that I did not notice when she came to perch on the edge of the sofa behind me. And then she started to speak.

In the months following my birth, she began, she had struggled to feel a connection to me. While she was pregnant, she'd thought that she'd been carrying a boy, and that he would emerge with a head of jet-black curls like hers. Instead, she got me, nine pounds and twelve whole ounces of blue-eyed blonde, a chunky miniature of my father. I paused what I was doing and turned to face her. *What was happening?* And it had been so hot, she continued, so very, swelteringly *hot*, that blazing summer of 1976, that I'd wriggled to be put down whenever she'd tried to hold me. *Where was this coming from?* When my brother was born, it was different, she went on. She smiled then, looking down at hands weathered and worn from the labor of loving us, remembering. The first time she'd looked him in the eyes, it was like she already knew him.

I swallowed hard, a sensation like cracked earth turning to dust in the space between my shoulder blades. Then I pushed back from my desk and stood abruptly up, propelled by a whirring ball of rage that had formed in the middle of my chest. *"Why are you telling me this?"* I croaked. *"Get away from me!"* I shouted, as she started to follow me into the kitchen. There I stood facing her, gripping the gray Formica countertop. By now I was sobbing. Who was she, this hateful person? Why was she here? *What, exactly, was she trying to say?* Through the white noise that was filling my skull I heard her telling me, *"I'm sorry, my sweet girl, I am so sorry."* But when she reached out for me, I pulled away. "Please get away from me," I told her again. Through my sobs, it came out "gawa'me." I gulped down some air and asked her again: *"Why are you telling me this?"* But even in that moment, part of me could see that she was giving me a gift.

In families like mine, where silence is the dysfunction, honesty—the *truth*—is the medicine. And while the room spun and her face went in and out of focus, one clear thought cut through the chaos in my head: *I knew it I knew it I knew it.* I had always known that the bond she had with my brother was on a different plane to what she felt for me, and finally hearing her say it felt like such a fucking relief.

She was also daring to vocalize one of the ultimate unspeakables; the fact that the love between a mother and her child is often more fraught, more complex, and more challenging than it is supposed to be. But given what we've seen about how hard it is to be a mom—from the personal sacrifices made, to a lack of material support, to the unrealistic expectations placed on mothers—*how could it not be?* Within the institution of patriarchal motherhood, every woman is assured that she will be consumed with cozy maternal feelings as soon as her infant child is placed upon her chest. Now, my own mother was lovingly clarifying for me that this is not always the case. That sometimes there is no magical immersion into milky bliss; just the creeping sensation that *I'm not sure I can handle this.*

Imagine if this were part of the overarching narrative about everything it means to be a mom. How might this impact our reproductive choices and our feelings about being women without kids? I was both surprised and not surprised at all at how many respondents to my survey cited strained relations with their own mother as one of their reasons for not wanting or having children of their own. What are your earliest recollections of being mothered? How do you remember it being for your mom, and in what ways might this have influenced how you feel about becoming a mother yourself? Of course, not everybody reading will be able to relate. But how can a person's experience of being mothered *not* impact how they feel about becoming a mother themselves?

Not that I am looking to "blame" my mother for the fact I never wanted kids; there is nobody to blame for anything, because no crime has been committed. Rather, with the autumn light streaming through my kitchen window, picking out fractals of wounded feelings that had been festering for decades, it felt like she was handing me a missing puzzle piece. If I have always felt like an outsider, as if me being me was not enough, then in a roundabout way, she was letting me know that there was nothing wrong with me, and there never had been. Also, that it was perfectly okay for me to be a woman without kids. As such, our exchange that brittle autumn day became another vital part of me *accepting* the life that has been mine to live—and the ways it has been shaped by both the culture at large and my family of origin.

The practice of acceptance speaks to our willingness to accept reality exactly as it is. Regardless of our reasons, I believe this concept is front and center for any woman without kids, and I want us to do a deep dive into it here. Not conforming to the selfless ideal of motherhood means accepting being seen as different, and it means accepting being judged. It means accepting being seen as *selfish cunts* while accepting that we will never "have it all." It means accepting every choice we've ever made that has led to us not having kids, and it means accepting the circumstances behind these choices. It might mean accepting having been less than "perfectly" mothered. Above all, it means accepting that even the most positive and empowering choices can be a way of avoiding pain. It means accepting the sources of this pain. All of which is never *not* going to be a challenging and confronting process, but it must be part of our story. Because accepting all of this is how we quit wondering "what if?" Accepting who we are, and how we got to where we are today, is what frees us to just live.

* * *

When we choose to accept something, we consent to it having a place in our life, no matter what. Which, whether a person, a situation, or an oppressive social stigma or regime, is easier said than done. In the immediate aftermath of her confession, I was not ready to accept my mother: in fact, I wanted nothing to do with her. Once my sobbing had subsided, I became a cold slab of granite that deflected her attempts at reconciliation without a flinch. The next day I put her on the plane back to England feeling justified in having moved to another continent and placed an ocean-wide boundary between us. No more being the dutiful daughter or feeling guilty for not including her in my life; she didn't deserve it. But in the weeks that followed, and as the dust began to settle, I could see that in fact a portal for healing had opened up between us.

Over the coming years, we would go on to engage in a series of conversations that felt almost psychedelic in their intensity. Conversations during which hours would whirl past in a swirl of memories, stinging resentments, and family secrets. Riding the waves, we clung to each other like a pair of shipwreck survivors far out to sea.

It was during this time that I learned of the women in my lineage who had lost their babies, their husbands, their minds. My mother shared how lost and bewildered she'd felt at times as a first-time mom, having no mother to mother her in her mothering. How baffled and hurt she'd been by the fact I seemed not to need her, even as an infant. I'd begun sucking my thumb in utero, and my ability to self-soothe had felt like a rejection of her mothering. Now, I was getting a clearer picture of how it must have been for her. Becoming a mother was all she'd ever wanted— but the reality had found her struggling. A struggle that, naturally, might manifest in her ability to connect with me. And while I have no memory of that time, I was right there with her. Feeling all the feelings. Absorbing all the insecurity and the self-doubt deep into my developing being. And slowly and surely, over a period of several years, I began to excavate my deepest *why* of all for being a woman without kids: part of me had always known I did not want to relive this.

I also began to accept my mother for who she is: a resilient and resourceful *survivor* who had always done her best with the difficult hand that she'd been dealt. Accepting the ways in which this had impacted our dynamic, and no longer wanting or needing our story to have unfolded any differently, I began to feel a palpable shift in the bond between us; frayed cotton building to sturdy rope. It was six years later that I began calling her each week in the early days of the pandemic, by which point I was getting closer to being able to accept what comfort she *was* able to offer, rather than bristling at how much I felt she'd always needed me.

It is also no coincidence that this recovering of my relationship with my mother—and my ultimate acceptance of our relationship exactly as it is—coincided with my decision to remove alcohol from my life. When I'd started to drink heavily in my early twenties, booze had become my preferred *agent of pretense*. Because that's what alcohol does. In numbing our feelings, severing us from reality, and muddling our memories of why we feel the way we do, drinking our way through life allows us to pretend that everything is *fine*.

In my case, wrapping myself in a boozy bubble of dissociation had also helped me to pretend that my family was not my family, our dysfunction was not our dysfunction; it had helped me to pretend that I was *normal*. But my family made me who I am—and within this, alcohol had also become a barrier to me accepting *myself*. It was over this same period that I began experimenting with longer and longer periods of abstinence. Windows in time during which a newfound clarity flooded my life. At first, the light was blinding, scorching my retinas with too much awareness delivered all at once. Sometimes, basking in it felt like its own kind of high. But as I grew more accustomed to the brightness, I began to peer curiously into what had been the darkest corners of my existence to see what I might find. Which, it turns out, was a neat little lineup of the grisly *home truths* I had spent my whole life trying to avoid.

There was my overall lack of self-worth, and my craving for external validation—manifesting in me chasing the career success that I'd *always put before family*; there were the constant money worries that equally drove my workaholism and my overachieving; and there was my fury at both my parents for not having teamed up all those years ago and told Adam to *back the fuck off*. Uglier and harder to stomach was my having zero remorse about having had an abortion, and what this said about me as a person; my inability and unwillingness to form a connection with my brother Joseph; and the intense guilt I felt about not even *wanting* to be a better daughter.

In fact, now that I was feeling all my feelings, it was impossible to ignore the fact that visits with my blood relatives often felt like they required me to hold my breath and zip something up tight on the inside. I was used to drinking over this stifling sensation; now I needed to know *why* I felt this way. And now that my mind was focused and clear, it was impossible to ignore the gaping holes where certain memories should have been: never having been hugged by any one of my grandparents; never having gone to either of my parents for advice or emotional support; there never having been a conversation about the impact of Joseph's condition on the wider family system.

Which is *a lot*, isn't it? But we all harbor experiences, thoughts, and feelings that we'd rather not acknowledge. What are your *home truths*, the parts of your story that it is harder to look at and the parts of yourself that it is not so easy to accept? If you're anything like the women in my survey, chances are that when you take a step back and begin to join the dots, many of these things will have factored into you being a woman without kids.

Perhaps most shocking of all to me was the *envy* that crept up on me when I was around children whose parents were loving and attentive with them. Jesus! Did you hear what I just said? I was *jealous* of *kids* for having parents who very evidently adored them. It wasn't long before I had to ask myself (like that therapist had tried to ask of me): what *did* all of this have to say about my own lack of desire to be a mom? My not wanting kids had never felt like a problem, but it was only now that I was beginning to realize it had also been a solution: not having a child would mean not creating new ties with my family of origin. In some ways, it was its own kind of estrangement from them. And if this was the case, where did my desire for autonomy and self-authorship end, and my rejection of my origin story begin?

The answer to this lay somewhere in the gap between the high-octane party/career-girl existence I had created for myself and the hollow void on the inside where the sanctuary of a loving and supportive family should have been. Not that becoming aware of any of this changed how I felt about not being a mom. As the alcoholic fog continued to be burnt off by the intensity of my inner inquiry, my conviction that this was the right path for me only felt clearer and truer. Nothing about the daily labor of mothering was a fit for my personality or my talents. But learning more about my mother's story had also helped me see the burdens that are placed on moms more clearly. As such, I began to acknowledge and accept that my Affirmative No was as much a rejection of the kinds of challenges she had faced as it was a yes to a different kind of life entirely.

As these home truths landed for me, I was able to find a new level of acceptance for the parts of myself that had always felt defective or less-than for being nobody's mom. Instead of trying to fearfully deny or push these parts away, I decided to invite them in and ask them *why* they felt the way they did. And slowly, I began to accept the whole truth of being a woman without kids: the autonomy *and* the otherness; the empowerment *and* the boxes that would go unchecked; the freedom *and* the fear of aging and dying alone. No amount of Instagram memes reminding me of all the money I'd saved, all the trips I could take, and all the long-suffering side-eye I was entitled to direct at strung-out breeders and their obnoxious toddlers could have helped me feel this way. I could only have gotten here by stepping back and taking a clear-eyed inventory of every aspect of my life—of our lives, as women who have come of age in the death throes of patriarchy.

Which is when I knew I had to write this book.

Why? I was also starting see that there was nothing wrong with being a woman without kids, and everything wrong with the unexamined assumption that every woman should want to be a mother. This despite glaring discrepancies between senti-mental portrayals of the role and our actual lived experiences of family life. Within this, I needed us to start talking about precisely what we are rejecting, and why, when we reject the selfless ideal of motherhood. I wanted to voice my gratitude for the progress that has enabled women to live the lives we want *and* my grief for the families we will never have when we don't have kids.

I also suspected, despite an increasingly vocal movement to legitimize the path of non-motherhood, that I was not the only woman cheering at posts championing our right to be childfree while also nursing secret feelings of resentment, alienation, and self-doubt. Who had struggled to find my full self within the two-dimensional caricatures of women without kids. The healing I'd done with my own mother had shown me what's possible when we're able to acknowledge and accept the whole truth of who we are. Now I began to wonder what it would mean for our unsung sisterhood, to borrow from that doyenne of selfish cunts, Virginia Woolf, "To look life in the face, always, to look life in the face, and to know it for what it is . . . at last, to love it for what it is, and then, to put it away."

* * *

As stated in the introduction to this book, my intention here has been threefold. In the first instance, I wanted to help join the dots between our personal reasons for being women without kids and the wider influences that have shaped our humanity. In doing so, I hope I have proved to you that no matter what your reasons for being nobody's mom, there is nothing wrong with you: if anything, there is everything *right* with pursuing life-paths that deviate from the patriarchal ideal-normal. By seeking to help validate and legitimize the path of non-motherhood, I also hope that any shame and alienation you may have experienced along the way is beginning to be replaced by a sense of *sisterhood*.

And now here we are, meeting at the dark, thorny heart of the labyrinth. At the top of this chapter I explained that accepting the totality of our reality is never not going to be a messy, painful, and confronting process—which also quite accurately describes my experience of completing this book. It has taken me to places I never saw coming, and to places where, intuitively, I knew we'd have to go. But whatever has come up for you thus far, it was never my intention to plunge us into an ice bath of awareness for the harsher factors that have shaped our lives as women without kids, and then just *leave us there*, flailing about and wondering where the fuck we are supposed to go from here.

Which is where the concept of acceptance comes in. Until we are able to accept reality exactly as it is, it's like we are forever boxing shadows. We know we're hurting, but for as long as we deny or willfully ignore the root cause of our pain, our efforts to heal and move beyond it will be futile. Likewise, continuing to fight against something that can or will not change will just wear us down and out. Accepting this something fully, however, is what allows us to detach from it, lay down our arms, and tend to our wounds instead. It is what creates the space for us to breathe and to regroup, the better to redirect our energy toward building *the lives of our dreams*. And not "dreams" in the cheesy Hallmark sense; more in a "well, this is fucked, so let's dream up something *better*" kind of a way.

For example, every woman without kids who has ever felt less than, or been told that her life is somehow incomplete, will have to accept that in a pronatalist society womanhood will *always* be synonymous with motherhood. To the extent that every woman *will be* expected to take mothering in her stride, without instruction, without adequate support, and without complaint. Any woman who "fails" at this, or who simply opts out, will also have to accept being branded as deviant and/or defective by those who benefit the most from the upholding of the status quo.

And here's the thing: *we don't have to agree with something— let alone like it—in order to accept it*. Rather, not needing it to be something it's not simply frees up energy, inspiration, and creativity. Allows us to retrain our focus on what it is we want to invite more of into our life, and to start actively pursuing these things for ourselves and as role models for others in our position. It's a vision that conjures the words of author Thornton Wilder: "I not only bow to the inevitable. I am fortified by it."

But what does the practice of acceptance look like in our lives? And when it comes to accepting dysfunctional family dynamics, and/or outright abuses of power, where do we draw the line?

First of all, acceptance is often something we have to learn, like a language. This is because accepting things, and people, as they are requires us to step outside of conditioned reactions, prejudices, and avoidance tactics that have been laid down over lifetimes, that are often part of our emotional inheritance. This in turn means slowing down, paying attention, and noticing where we're operating on autopilot, burying our head in the sand, or holding back from voicing an inconvenient truth. This process can be equal parts vulnerable, daunting, and discomforting. Taking the neural pathway less traveled requires literal cognitive effort, and where our default responses are also coping mechanisms (people pleasing or self-medicating rather than speaking our truth, for example) it may also mean wading through all kinds of wounding that we'd rather not look at.

What are some of the changes and the challenging conversations you might need to instigate to begin living closer to your truth as a woman without kids? What might you need to accept about your life, and the world in general, in order to confront these things head-on?

I believe my mother was actively practicing acceptance with me on that fateful day. For her part, she has since shared that she knew she had to attempt to close the gap that existed between us. What she had to work with was her truth, which in subsequent conversations has led to a deeper understanding on both our parts about why we had often struggled to connect. By quitting pretending that everything was *fine*, she was accepting the reality of our imperfect mother-daughter bond. By giving a voice to the part of her that had felt defective in her mothering, she was practicing self-acceptance. By sharing this with me, she was asking me to accept her for who she is, and to accept her love as she had been able to offer it. On a deeper level, in opening the vaults of our shared ancestry, she was also giving me an opportunity to accept my place in our troubled lineage.

Not that I was ready to accept any of this in the moment. Because the messed-up part, and what often gets in the way of acceptance, is that sometimes it *validates our suffering* for everything to be fucked and for the world to be against us. Having something or someone to rail against can also become a person's raison d'être, not least because fighting against a perceived enemy can be a lot less complicated than putting in the protracted, humbling effort of peacemaking, consensus building, or creating an alternative way of doing things from scratch. Which is what my mother and I embarked on in the years that followed—a project that is ongoing.

Considering everything I've shared, what are some of the things that you are being asked to accept as part of being a woman without kids? Maybe, like myself and many of the women in my survey, it is the traumas experienced by the women—and particularly the mothers—in your lineage, and the emotional inheritance you carry from this. Perhaps it is pressure from family and the wider society to hurry up and have a kid already. Maybe it is other people's opinions about the fact you don't have kids; gaslighting about the realities of patriarchal motherhood; or being made to feel guilty for not fulfilling your procreative duty. Perhaps it is being seen as selfish, shallow, sad, and immature, or as cold and overly ambitious for prioritizing your career. Maybe it is the fact you have not been able to get pregnant, that you haven't met the right person to co-parent with, the prohibitive cost of IVF, or how hard it is to adopt a kid.

In the name of dismantling the Mommy Binary (which, I'll say it again, is one of the most toxic, divisive, and pervasive threats to a fully liberated womankind), it is important to acknowledge that mothers must accept much of the above, too. These are things that women and woman-identifying individuals in general are made to accept under pronatalist patriarchy, and becoming a mom does not exempt one from being subject to them.

Perhaps most important of all, when it comes to accepting any and all of the above, we also can't skip over the part where we *feel all our feelings* about whatever is present for us as a result. Writing about accepting her own childlessness, the novelist Marian Keyes noted, "It's impossible to go from fear and discomfort to acceptance. Other emotions need to be felt and expressed—rage, grief, denial, depression—before any kind of acceptance becomes remotely possible."[45]

Have any of these emotions come up for you while reading this book? Regardless of your experience of being a woman without kids—or of mothering and being mothered—it's likely that some of what's been uncovered in these pages has brought up similar feelings of anger, despair, and, yes, even grief. Not least, perhaps, for what Adrienne Rich calls "the mutilation and manipulation [by patriarchal motherhood] of the relationship between mother and child, which is the great original source and experience of love."

The hardest part of all? We also have to accept that there are some things we have zero control over, and which we therefore have *no option* but to accept exactly as they are—regardless of the pain they may have caused us or others. This includes any and all past events, including things that have happened to us personally and world events. Also, other people: how they feel, what they think, and the actions that they take. Most relevant to our conversations here, this includes our primary caregivers and the way they chose (or had no option but) to raise us. Also, the politicians, dictators, and corporate robber-bandits who benefit the most from the perpetuation of domination systems. Which brings me back to the question of where we draw the line about what it is okay to accept.

For example, accepting abusive parents for who they are will likely mean putting some hardcore boundaries in place—an essential part of what Marine Sélénée calls "moving from blind love to enlightened love." When we love somebody blindly, as is often the case with family since we are biologically wired to remain loyal to them, "we sacrifice our own good in order to belong." When we are able to transition to a place of enlightened love, however, "We don't sacrifice our higher good to placate or please others. . . . We accept reality and we accept what is beyond our power to control: other people." Meanwhile, letting go of who we think our parents "should" be can be a powerful step toward accepting the one thing they have surely given us: the gift of life itself. Sélénée also notes that accepting her own mother's imperfect mothering was "immensely liberating, because I stopped holding myself to a standard I could never meet."

And what about the wider structural injustices that have impacted our shared humanity throughout the ages; are we supposed to accept these too? My grisly sobbing that day in the kitchen has been matched in intensity by the tears I've wept while working on this book; the upwelling of anger I projected at my mother revealed as the overflow from a river of sadness surging beneath the surface. Anger at the injustices done by domination systems; sadness for all the unnecessary suffering this has caused. Looking back, my reaction to her confession also seems extreme. But there's a saying: when it's hysterical, it's historical. Had the visceral eruption of rage even been mine? Or had it, in fact, belonged to all the women of my ancestry, all women everywhere, whose bodies, whose mothering, and whose choices have been so manhandled under centuries of patriarchy?

There is no denying that the history of our humanity has been messy and bloody and full of inequities. In a way, more women without kids is the logical endgame of this lineage, given that centuries of exploitation of people and planet have resulted in social, economic, and environmental conditions that are simply not supportive of child-rearing and family life. And are not supportive of a thriving humanity overall. Ultimately, though, we have no option but to accept this, too—the better to steady our focus on the things that we *can* change, which are the choices we make, the actions we take, and our perceptions of our current circumstances. Now, we are back in the driver's seat, and we are ready to begin the work of building an *other* legacy, which we will examine in depth in the final chapter. Nothing that has been done can be undone. But only when we are able to accept our life today, exactly as it is, do we actually get to *live* it.

* * *

The other thing about acceptance? It makes us somewhat impervious to regret; the oft-cited notion that women without kids will *regret* not becoming parents delivering the ultimate in existential FOMO. How does it feel in your body when you hear this? More like a threat than a loving reminder, right? Orna Donath describes this as "a politicized use of emotion," since the fear it evokes is designed to get us back with the pronatalist program. But when we can accept who we are, and why, we are less likely to regret the choices we have made. We are also more likely to have empathy and understanding for the person who made those choices. Looking ahead, making a commitment to accepting whatever life brings also becomes its own insurance policy against life's inevitable challenges, disappointments, and setbacks.

And besides, what about the ones *who regret having kids*? Why don't we ever let them have their say? The subject of Donath's groundbreaking study is one of the edgiest societal taboos, the thorniest of all home truths. And yet surveys conducted over the past decade in the United States, the United Kingdom, Germany, and Poland put the number of people who regret having become parents at between 7 and 14 percent—a not insignificant cohort. Given the unspeakable nature of *this* topic, it's likely that these numbers are also underreported. Meanwhile, experts quoted in a 2021 *Atlantic* article on the subject cite two main causes of parental regret: parental burnout and *not wanting kids in the first place.*[46] Which means, if in doubt . . . perhaps don't.

And then there are the older women without kids I have encountered while writing this book—not one of whom told me she regretted her choice not to become a mom. If it has been a choice, that is. I have met involuntarily childless women, for example, who regret having had an abortion when they were younger. My successful artist friend, meanwhile, regrets not prioritizing having kids. But surely you are less likely to regret an action not taken than a deed that cannot be *undone*—like, say, bringing a whole new human into the world, whose existence and well-being you will remain responsible for on some level for the rest of your life.

Reflecting on this, I am reminded of a powerful sentiment from *Regretting Motherhood.* Writing about women who decide to share their regrets with their kids, Donath notes: "To protect their children from possibly making the same mistakes, they must share with them the distresses that might accompany motherhood, the idea that it might not be worthwhile, and the reassurance that it is a legitimate decision to 'opt out.'"

Not that my mother was telling me that she *regretted* having me when she shared her truth that day. In fact, I'm pretty sure she would be appalled by the suggestion; being a mum to my brother and me has been the defining experience of her life. But her honesty about the reality of the role was clarifying. She had been built for motherhood, had wanted it with every part of her being, and even she had struggled. In my case, I'd had to work to cobble together the semblance of desire for a child; undoubtedly, it would be even harder for a woman like me, as for any woman who orients closer to the Affirmative No end of the Motherhood Spectrum, to reconcile the sentimental fantasy with the monotonous, sleep-deprived reality.

Knowing what you know about yourself and your life, and accepting this in its wholeness, do you think you are more likely to regret not having a child, or to regret becoming a mom? This might feel like a leading question, given the subject matter of this book. But it might well be that having come this far, and having dug deeper into all the factors impacting our unsung sisterhood, that it's the former. In which case, this is your invitation to begin actively prioritizing becoming a mom yourself, or finding other ways to mother in your life. Also, to continue to work on accepting your life exactly as you find it, along with the circumstances that have led you here.

Recent taboo-busting conversations about both parental burnout and regret are helping to lessen the stigma surrounding these topics. Ditto with postpartum depression (PPD)—another subject that always held a lurid fascination for me, and something else that made me question the notion that I would inevitably regret not having kids. How was it that what was supposed to be the most joyful period in a woman's life could also plunge her into a cold, dark well of despair, and even trigger psychosis? Wasn't this more evidence that not *all women* naturally morph into perfectly selfless and capable mothers once they have a child?

The latest statistics show that PPD affects around 15 percent of new moms in the United States, while in a post for her Evolutionary Parenting blog, educator Tracy Cassels asked: "Is Post-Partum Depression a Modern-Day Problem?" In addition to hormonal factors, she argues, a person experiencing PPD can equally be attributed to the impact of industrialization (and within this, patriarchal motherhood) on modern parenting practices. An increase in cesarean sections, early separation between a mother and her newborn, the erasure of postpartum rituals, a lack of practical and emotional support from her immediate community, economic hardship, insufficient parental leave, and modern sleep practices (i.e., the infant sleeping in a separate room, making it harder for new moms to manage night feedings), have all been shown to increase the risk of PPD. As has the *loss of identity* that can accompany motherhood: the fact that, for all her education, her hopes, her dreams, and her career success, once she births a child she is now primarily seen as somebody's mom. The latter being a consideration that has only arisen in the aftermath of the women's liberation movement.

Cassels also makes an important point that speaks directly to the concept of acceptance: "focusing all our attention on fixing a problem instead of *preventing* the problem seems wrong to me." In the case of PPD, prevention begins first and foremost with women feeling fully supported in their mothering—which in turn means accepting the unfair burdens that are currently placed on mothers. Only when we can see these clearly can we see how important it is for our communities, our workplaces, and our governments to prioritize support for mothers and families.

But as we now know, the systemic issues that have eroded this support run centuries deep. And while we can't *undo* the harms that women and children have experienced as a result, we can do our best to prevent more harm from continuing to be done. In the meantime, "preventing" the problems associated with both parental regret and PPD might well mean *not having kids*. Might again find a person making a realistic assessment of their parental readiness—whether consciously or intuitively—that takes *all* the factors impacting moms today into account.

For some, making this evaluation and accepting that you may never be ready to be a mother in this life might lead to a period of intense grieving. Not that experiencing sadness about not having kids means you can't *also* be confident in the choice not to pursue parenthood. It's okay to grieve something you will never have *and* to feel empowered in your decision to prioritize other things. If anything, as Jeanne Safer writes in *Beyond Motherhood*, "To acknowledge that you are unwilling or unable to undertake everything a woman is now supposed to is sober, realistic, and an enormous relief." The real relief comes from accepting whatever fears and limitations might find us orienting toward the Affirmative No end of the Motherhood Spectrum and focusing instead on where our desires and capacities might lead us.

Honestly? The only things I've regretted were the results of choices I've made that were not a 100 percent Affirmative, orgasmic YES for me. These regrets range from little lies I've told myself and others, to purchases I've made, to projects I've invested time and energy in that were not in full integrity with the person I strive to be. Perhaps my greatest regret is writing my real phone number on the back of that beer coaster in Amsterdam's Bulldog Café. And while I regret the harm done to myself and my psyche in that relationship, I also *accept* it as an essential part of my story. Not least for the primary lesson it taught me, which was to never, *ever* not trust my instincts again. That if it wasn't a "hell yes" then it had to be a *no*. What past actions or choices, if any, do you actively regret? And what would it take for you to accept these experiences as part of who you are today?

Personally, I have never regretted something I *haven't* done. This is partly because I've been privileged enough to be able to pursue the things I have wanted for myself: education, immigration, travel, creativity, a relationship with the person of my choosing, and a career that allows me to utilize my innate gifts. All of which has been easier for me to pursue *because I am a woman without kids*. But living a life of no regrets is also the result of the work I continue to do to accept my myself, my home truths, and my life today. Right here, right now, exactly as I am. Work that helps me to accept that while I might not have it all, I have everything I need, and more. To accept that this is enough.

"

"I do feel, a little bit, that if I don't have kids I must have a great career. I don't like that pressure. I'm trying to shift into questions like, did I enjoy my time on earth? Did I see the places I want to see, did I spend time with folks I love, did I find peace? Did I create art that I wanted to create, did I express myself? I think shifting what it means to me to be alive has helped me with the pressure I feel."

— age thirty-five, in a relationship

"Everything I do, pretty much, is trying to make good use of the time I wasn't able to sink into kids, and reach other humans with the same energy."

— age forty-nine, single

"I am Native American, and passing on my culture and bloodline is one of the biggest things swaying me towards having children."

— age thirty-eight, married

"

flashes; why did nobody talk about what Sheehy described as "a sense of . . . exultation [as if] the crystals of creative energy were flowing in reverse—from womb to mind" that permeated a woman's life after the storms had abated? And as for no longer being beholden to one's children's needs? I felt myself flooded with gratitude for the fact that as a woman without kids I had had the freedom to direct the lion's share of my energy toward whatever called to me for *my entire life*.

By this point, people had given up asking me why I didn't want kids. I assumed that they assumed I'd either tried and failed to get pregnant or was one of those odd creatures who had simply *missed the point*. Either way, best to just leave her to it. And it was only now, wrapped in a towel to guard against the chill that had been ushered onto the sand by the gradually setting sun, that I realized I could say with absolute confidence that I had zero regrets about being nobody's mom. Rather than pressing a panic button in my uterus, Sheehy's book had left me *looking forward* to menopause, as I contemplated all the things that I might do with my own second adulthood.

What a *selfish cunt*. This was the moment when the original title for this book downloaded into my brain, as if I'd made a selection from the Big Ideas vending machine in the sky. SELFISH CUNT. Along with the awkward otherness I'd always felt about being a woman without kids, this was the first time I became fully aware of the *guilt* I'd also harbored about not having dedicated my life to nurturing and raising a child. Which was just so fucked up, wasn't it? My decision not to become a mom had not hurt anybody. If anything, it meant I could be available for my partner, my family, and my wider community—while still having time for *me*. For my own creativity and healing. This wasn't selfish: it had been vital for my well-being and my sanity. It was also the life Sheehy described for all women postmenopause: "Women who no longer belong to somebody [i.e., their children] now can belong to everybody—the community, a chosen circle of friends, a worship group, or even to the world—by virtue of contributing knowledge or creative insight or healing gifts."

What if this had been the message that I had internalized from the culture all along, instead of it being implied that my nulliparous life meant there was *something wrong with me?* What if the path of non-motherhood had always been presented as being equally valid to that of motherhood? What if the circumstances and motivations behind any woman not becoming a mom were acknowledged and accepted in all of their complexity? Watching the clouds on the horizon turn from fluffy white to pink tiger stripes and then to molten gold, the embryo of my new project began to form.

The result is the book you are holding in your hands, or listening to, right now. The two-plus years I have spent researching and writing on this subject have helped me weave the threads of my personal story into something both cohesive and complete. As painful as this has been at times, the result is that I feel more at home with my choice than ever. Not being a mom makes sense to me on every level: familial, societal, and spiritual. At the same time, I feel more connected to the other women without kids *and* the mothers in my life, including my own mum, and to the things that unite us as women first and foremost. Widening the aperture to take in our collective experiences of mothering and being mothered has also helped me orient myself and my life in the historical arc of womankind—a process that has been as confronting as it has been inspiring. Never again will I take for granted the decades, the *centuries*, of resistance that have made it possible for me to choose the kind of life I want to live. Never again will I not remember my responsibility to pay this forward. Our responsibility for this, as we join together in sisterhood.

Which brings us to the final topic that I want us to consider here: what will our legacy be when we don't have kids?

In legal terms, "legacy" speaks to material inheritance—any money or property that is left to a person's descendants or other beneficiaries in a will. This in and of itself raises questions as to who, if not our children, will survive us after we are gone. Turning the corner of midlife had also found me looking my own mortality in the face; the feeling, as I contemplated how my final days would play out, like finishing a novel and finding a blank page where the ending was supposed to be. To whom *would* I leave my raggedy collection of paperbacks and vintage designer shoes? Who would carry out my instructions about what to do with my body? If I even had a funeral, who would read my eulogy? With no living, breathing embodiment of my genes to carry the torch, when I was gone, I would be *gone*.

But legacy is about so much more than the physical things we leave behind. In a spiritual sense, leaving an "other" legacy speaks more to the memories we make with our loved ones, the positive (and likely unknown) impact of our words and actions on the lives of others, and any and all creative offerings we might contribute along the way. When it comes to our individual origin stories and the planet on which we live, it could also be said to include *what we can clean up while we're here*, doing what we can, that is, to leave our little corner of the world nice and neat and tidy for whoever will come along to fill it. None of which requires us to have children of our own—and all of which is the natural by-product of us knowing who we are, discovering what makes life meaningful to us, and actually living the lives we have been given. This, I believe, is what Sheehy was encouraging her readers to lean in to with her talk of a "second adulthood." And regardless of your age today, it is never too early or too late for any woman without kids to consider what her other legacy might be.

* * *

Let's begin by looking at the "creative offerings" piece. The human instinct to create—that is, to apply head, heart, and hands to the task of shaping the world around us into something more useful or beautiful than when we found it—is universal. But most of us don't think of ourselves as creative beings. When we think of "creative" endeavors, we tend to go straight to the arts: music, sculpture, painting, poetry. Perhaps this expands to creative professions, such as writing, photography, and design, or discovery- and "solution-" oriented careers in the sciences or technology—pursuits and career paths that are also seen as inaccessible to most. You are born with a natural talent or gift, and/or the kind of connections that mean you can get paid for your creative output; you've got rich parents or other benefactors to pay the bills while you tinker away at your next *oeuvre*; or you possess the single-mindedness and other resources to dedicate years of your life to pursuing your Big Idea.

But the truth is, we are all born creative: when you think about it, we're making stuff all the time. We make breakfast, we make lists, we make friends. We make conversation, we make each other laugh, and we make mistakes. We make love, and yes, we make babies. The latter often is seen as the pinnacle of creativity, especially for women: *what greater act of creation is there than to create life?* But thinking about creativity in a broader sense, especially in terms of how our creative efforts might be part of an other legacy, brings to mind another concept highlighted in Aurélie Athan's paper on reproductive identity: that of *generativity*.

Developmental psychologist Erik Erikson, who broke ground in the 1950s with his theory about the nine stages of psychosocial development, identified generativity as an inherent need in all humans to contribute to and improve the lives of others by "establishing and guiding the next generation."[47] Generativity involves answering the question "Can I Make My Life Count?," with researchers in the 1990s expanding the definition to include a concern for one's legacy, referred to as an "inner desire for immortality" (i.e., to leave a lasting imprint with our existence). And interestingly, Erikson also claimed that generativity is what defines the seventh stage of life: ages forty through sixty-five, a time period that encompasses the peak of a woman's child-rearing years, menopause, and her transition to her second adulthood. For any woman without kids, regardless of how she feels about it, this is also the life stage when she will need to make her peace with being nobody's mom.

But there is nothing to say that a person can't engage with their generativity earlier in life—especially if children have not been the main focus of the sixth life stage, ages eighteen through forty, which orients around relationships, love, and intimacy. Meanwhile, Athan points out that "while parenthood was depicted as an important source, Erikson did not consider offspring necessary for achieving generativity." Further, she writes, "Theorists since have broadened its various forms: biological (bearing), parental (nurturing), technical (teaching), cultural (creating), and societal (mentoring), and found them all to be associated with well-being, opportunity for reinvention, and a second chance at life." This suggests that not only is orienting one's life in any way, shape, or form toward generativity a way to have a positive impact on the lives of others, it can also be part of our own healing and personal growth.

So, how can you determine what engaging your generativity might look like for you? Honestly, you're probably already doing it—or at least eyeing it from a distance, like the glittering pot of gold at the end of a rainbow-colored road of adventure and possibility. I'm pretty sure that anybody who's picked up this book has questioned whether having a kid is supposed to be the be-all-and-end-all of what they have to offer and has felt some sort of a pull toward other expressions of what this might be. Perhaps this is already reflected in what you do for a living, or perhaps it has manifested in a thriving passion project. Maybe it shows up in your relationships and in the community activities you facilitate. It could also be beckoning to you in the form of a research project or an artistic outlet. Reflecting on this, in what ways are you already engaging with your generativity, in your work, in your relationships, and with your creative endeavors? How could you build on this going forward?

Key to thinking about these things in terms of generativity is that the term also sounds a lot like "generous activity"; in some way, shape, or form, acts of generativity have the potential to benefit others. Meanwhile, it is often the challenges we have overcome in our own lives that show us what we have to offer, the lessons learned and any wisdom gained along the way being precisely what we are now qualified to pass along. Sometimes, we may find ways to offer these life lessons in more traditional formats—books, workshops, coaching sessions, or official mentorships. Especially if we identify as what Athan calls "cultural parents": CEOs, entrepreneurs, and other individuals who take it upon themselves to shape and guide the culture (and who definitely don't have to be biological parents). And other times, us being unapologetically us might be all it takes to touch and inspire others.

Crucially, however, generativity was defined by Erikson as the "ability to transcend personal interests to provide care and concern for younger and older generations." And given what we've learned about our lapsed societal duty of care, I believe this also extends to anybody who could be considered vulnerable, or whose needs and voices have been marginalized. For anybody who is serious about what it might mean to leave an other legacy, this means asking ourselves how we can employ our generativity in direct support of mothers, children, minority groups, people with disabilities, sick people, and the elderly. Not because we should, or because it makes us look good, but because this is how we start to play our part in creating a more equitable world.

Not that any of this applies solely to women without kids, and not that non-parents necessarily have an excess of time, money, or energy on their hands to put into altruistic projects. Even if, as one woman comments in *Regretting Motherhood* (referring to her time spent in online chatrooms for childfree women), "I find it irritating that everyone presumes that a demanding career or uninhibited hedonism are at the center of nonparents' lives. [Reading] this forum . . . music, philosophy, and volunteering, for instance, are the dominant topics here."

And not that supporting mothers and children, for example, has to mean working directly with kids—something, given the "nurturing," "teaching," and "mentoring" elements, we might think of as a necessary part of enacting generativity. But not all of us are *good with kids*. Myself included. When I finally found a therapist, ten years after my first failed attempt, one of the first things she asked on learning that I was a woman without kids was if I'd found other ways to connect with children in my life. "God no," I blurted. I was ashamed to admit it: "I don't like being around kids." Vocalizing this, I realized I'd always felt like this made me cold-hearted or a bad person. It was getting curious about all this that helped me uncover the root of the helpless self-consciousness that clung to me when I was in the presence of anybody under the age of ten—which was partly to do with my disavowal of my own "childish" parts, as I identified as part of my origin story.

But still, I am never going to be the friend who volunteers to chaperone your five-year-old's birthday party. And that's okay. A recent conversation with one new mom shed fresh light on what a generative contribution to her life might look like instead. While offering ourselves up for babysitting duties can be helpful in some cases, it can also be lazy, misguided thinking. She spelled it out: "Being a mom comes with tons of logistical, minute-to-minute childcare stuff. It would be impractical and inappropriate to ask my friends without kids for help with that." Instead, she encouraged me to "be the sister who's available for hikes, and coffee dates, and conversations about our careers and the wider culture, where it's more about our relationship as equals." Where she still gets to be *the woman she is without her kids*, she meant. And I am *great* at being that friend.

Engaging our generativity doesn't have to mean putting in long-suffering hours of servitude; often it will be the by-product of something that comes naturally to us, and which we enjoy doing. It might take effort, yes, and it may well mean going out of our way to consider what the most *generous activity* in any given situation might be. But there are as many iterations of generativity as there are people on the planet, the human experience overall being a melting pot of unique desires, capacities, fears, and limitations. As with the Motherhood Spectrum, some of us are more naturally suited to certain iterations of generativity than others. Yet another reminder that there is no one-size-fits-all approach to life, to the contributions we make, and to the ripple effect of whatever legacy is the result of the actions that we take.

* * *

But wait a minute. One thing I didn't want to do in this chapter is make it sound like women without kids owe a *debt to society* for not fulfilling their reproductive duty. That in lieu of producing any new humans we had better figure out an alternative way to leave a legacy and contribute something of value to the wider society. Ideally one that in some way resembles a cure for cancer or an international peace treaty. If anything, the message I am trying to convey here is that you just being you, but like, really *you*, is enough. But—what I am about to say in no way negating what I just said—at this juncture in our human story it is all of our duty to be asking what we can do to leave our planet in a better place than we currently find it. Parents and non-parents and everybody in between.

Perhaps the most important and the most challenging way to think about generativity is how we can apply this to the environmental mega-crisis that is set to define the twenty-first century. The endangered elephant that has been hovering over this text being: what kind of world are we leaving for future generations to inherit? In his 2020 documentary, *A Life on Our Planet*, ninety-three-year-old David Attenborough charts the environmental degradation he has witnessed over seven decades documenting the natural world. It is humbling, eerie viewing; watching the camera pan charred forest floors and oceans clogged with plastic feels like waking up from a drunken blackout in a strange, quiet house littered with overflowing ashtrays and broken glass. This is the mess that a centuries-long rager of overconsumption has created for current and future generations to clean up.

No wonder the kids are pissed and some of the most ardent birth dissenters, as quoted in Suzy Weiss's article on the radical childfree movement, cite it being "morally wrong to bring a child into the world." A world in which an unending stream of climate disasters is practically guaranteed, they mean. Since overpopulation is seen as the chief driver of overconsumption, and thus pollution and environmental ruin, the fact that "there are too many people in the world" is another oft-cited reason for abstaining from having kids. It came up frequently in my survey, and it's a position that is gaining traction. Meanwhile, at the end of his documentary, David Attenborough unveils his number-one "solution" to the climate catastrophe: to dramatically, and as swiftly as we can, slow down with the reproduction of the species.

But as also previously noted, this is a simplistic notion of a fix for what is a far more complex and long-range issue than the ethics of disposable diapers. For starters, conversations about population control are often tinged with xenophobia and racism. When demographers express concerns about women in India, Africa, and the Middle East continuing to have large families, this is often linked to climate change; more people in developing nations means greater ecological strain on parts of the world that are already suffering the most from pollution, extreme temperatures, and flooding. But how much of this "concern" is really rooted in fears about mass migration of Black and brown people, with their Black and brown cultures and religious beliefs, to the West? After all, women in white, Western nations are actively being encouraged to have more kids. Even when, under current conditions, a child born in an affluent nation such as the United States will be responsible for forty times the carbon emissions of a child born in Bangladesh.[48]

Fear of overpopulation also makes human beings the problem—when it is the systems that govern us, and the lifestyles they perpetuate, that are broken. This was the original message of the official BirthStrike movement, which was founded by women who, by announcing their decision not to have children, sought to draw attention to the horrors of environmental collapse—and the responsibility of governments and corporations to enact policies to address this. But the group disbanded in 2020, stating that they had "underestimated the power of 'overpopulation' as a growing form of climate breakdown denial."[49] Meaning, they had not foreseen the extent to which not having a kid would be used as a get-out-of-climate-change-free card by those unwilling to take a more actively political stance or make other lifestyle changes to address the issue.

The real "fix" is to dramatically reduce the carbon footprint overall, in Western nations especially. For example, people often talk about being free to travel as much as they like when they don't have kids. But in a 2018 column for Vox, economist Lyman Stone points out that just one extra vacation can rack up the same carbon footprint as a baby in its first year. If we are really concerned about the climate, we all know what to do: quit flying, go electric, eat vegan, recycle, recycle, recycle. Which we all know is also harder than it sounds.

I know I'm not the only person here who has vowed to commit to all of the above only to become disheartened and give up at the first hurdle. I'll take my reusable cup to get coffee and wonder "what's the point?" as I walk past trash cans overflowing with single-use plastic; I'll swear off Amazon Prime and then run out of time to travel across town to get the (definitely not plant-based) food my cat prefers; I choose to live in the United States and justify the air miles I rack up visiting my parents with the fact that I don't have kids.

Doing right by the climate is undoubtedly some of the most important legacy work we can do. But the sheer enormity of the issues that we face—impossible for our human brains to fully comprehend—versus what can feel like our pointless, drop-in-the-ocean efforts, makes it some of the hardest. Especially when coupled with an unwillingness from Big Government to match our individual efforts with decisive and radical action on deforestation and carbon emissions. What are the biggest blocks to you engaging with climate work? What do you think it would it take, both individually and in society at large, to overcome these blocks?

If anything, it makes sense that some of the most committed everyday climate activists I know are moms—since they are the ones with a living, breathing vested interest in safeguarding the future of the planet. When one deeply environmentally conscious friend was feeling torn up by her decision about whether to have a kid, she squared her ultimate choice to become a mom by making a pact with herself: she would double down on doing *all the things* when it came to living an environmentally ethical life. Watching her claim her Affirmative Yes about motherhood also made me believe there is a kernel of truth in something Jeanne Safer told me when we spoke: "I don't think anybody decides not to have a child *because* of climate change. It may factor into the equation, particularly for people who feel guilty about [not wanting to be a mom]—they can say, 'I'm doing this for the planet!'" When, in fact, "It's perfectly fine not to have a child because you don't want to be a mother. Period, the end. Don't feel you have to have an explanation that makes you a 'good person' in other ways."

Ultimately, Lyman Stone draws the conclusion that "the only hope for the climate is a quantum-leap breakthrough in carbon efficiency"—a leap that will require never-seen-before "technological, geographic, and social advancement." This reminds me of what adrienne maree brown calls "science fictional behavior." Part of her *Emergent Strategy*, an expansive and hopeful manifesto for social change that was the precursor to *Pleasure Activism*, engaging with science fictional behavior means striving to be the change that we cannot yet see, while at the same time "being concerned with how our beliefs now, today, will shape the future, tomorrow, the next generations." This means attuning not just our actions but also our *thinking* to generativity, since this is "how we intentionally change in ways that grow our capacity to embody the just and liberated worlds we long for . . . *to turn our legacy towards harmony* [emphasis mine]."

Harmony between beings—manifesting in global consensus on the issue of carbon emissions, for example—is key to enacting Big Picture solutions when it comes to climate. Harmony, consensus, and reciprocity, in turn, are the building blocks of mutually supportive partnership systems—and actually mimic the interdependent ecosystems of the natural world. Healing our estrangement from the universal mother,[50] Earth, ultimately lies in remembering that animals, trees, fungi, plants, insects, and algae are as much a part of our "family" as our human kinship groups. That these beings—trees and plants in particular, with their quiet, tireless photosynthesis of light into calories and their sequestering of carbon from the air we breathe—nurture and provide for us just as our human communities do. Within this remembering, we can begin to see that our legacy work and our duty of care equally extends to them. That the stakes of the environmental crises we face are not only existential, but moral.

* * *

Perhaps one of the biggest blocks to us grappling with the cataclysmic threat of climate change is that it requires us to envision the end of *our* world as we know it—and to accept that death is a natural part of life. This is something that Western cultures in particular have a notoriously difficult time with. Meanwhile, with no reference point for our own demise, and with no way of knowing how and when we will go, it is literally impossible for us to picture the reality of our own death. Some psychologists also believe that the denial of death is a vital psychic coping mechanism: if we spent each day fully present to the fact that every breath might be our last, we would become completely paralyzed.[51] Not only would we start seeing the grim reaper leering at us from around each corner, but when death is inevitable, what is the point of living?

Which is another reason people love babies, isn't it? Babies are bouncing, burbling proof that life always trumps death in the end. But how much of our disavowal of death is rooted in the fear that *we will not have lived* before our time is up? After all, according to multiple sources, the number-one deathbed regret goes something like: "I wish I'd had the courage to live a life true to myself, and not the life others expected of me."[52] I believe this sentiment speaks directly to the collective legacy of women without kids, which is to continue to legitimize the path of non-motherhood for future generations of women by modeling what it looks like to color outside the lines of what society expects of us. Especially as we age. When there is no "next generation" to pick up where we left off, it is on us to live our lives to the absolute fullest—and in doing so, to inspire others to do the same.

Given my predictions about the impact on the birth rate of the daughters of the women's liberation movement reaching the end of our reproductive years, we are also about to witness an insurgence of older, wiser ladies without babies. One day, you will be one of them. Regardless of the age you are today, how do you picture your own "second adulthood" playing out? When you picture your own death, who do you see at your bedside? What memories will you leave them with, and what other imprints will your existence leave behind?

In the introduction to this book, I shared how my game—*Does She Have Kids?*—was born from the fact that I have been looking for women-without-kids role models my entire life. Why? First and foremost, I wanted to know that it was okay for me not to have kids. But I also wanted to be inspired by others who had walked this path. I wanted evidence that not having a child would not mean my life had been for nothing, and I wanted to stop feeling guilty for pursuing the things that were an Affirmative Yes for me. Which is what I want for every woman without kids; not least so that we can quit wasting time wondering "what if?" and get on with engaging fully with alternative iterations of our creativity and our generativity instead.

In *The Silent Passage*, Gail Sheehy also speaks to the importance of developing an ideal "future self" in the mind's eye when envisioning a positive experience of aging: "The more clearly we visualize [her], admire her indomitable skeleton and the grooves of experience that make up the map of her face, the more comfortable we will be with moving into her container." But my life being so different from that of my mother and my grandmothers, and with a lack of alternative women-without-kids role models in my life, it had always been difficult to picture "little old me." Which touches on another important piece that every woman without kids is poised to disrupt as part of enacting an other legacy: that unless you are somebody's grandma, Western society has *no place for old women.*

This places additional pressure on women to have kids as a way to valorize our mothers—the archetype of the grandmother, waiting just beyond the hump of menopause, being the only valid and respectable embodiment of *wise woman energy*. If anything, the grandma is the most sentimentalized of all the feminine gender roles—the child-full matriarch to the child-less witch. Having fulfilled her procreative duty, and then some, she has more than earned her keep in the collective consciousness, where she is revered as the fount of all nurturance. Doling out endless kisses and bowls of chicken soup for the soul, to disrespect grandma is blasphemy. Even if, should grandma take it upon herself to lay down her knitting needles and exert her influence in the sphere of public life, she will often find she is quickly put back in her place. A recent pantomime-like example being Hillary Clinton's 2016 presidential bid at age seventy: *LOCK THAT NASTY WOMAN UP*.

I have written the bulk of this manuscript in a cabin in the woods in upstate New York. It belongs to my friend Shauna, a hypnotherapist, and my only company while I'm here is her collection of esoteric books and her little black cat. It couldn't get much witchier, to be honest, the stereotype of the witch—that ancient, reviled symbol of fully autonomous womanhood being perhaps the most pervasive image we have for the archetype of the crone, or wise woman. And in fairytales, none of the witches have kids. In fact, they are often depicted eating young children and putting curses on pubescent girls. Elsewhere, the "childless elderwoman" (as Jody Day would have it) who finds companionship and solace in a beloved pet is "the crazy cat lady"; the older women who expresses her sexuality beyond her childbearing years is a predatory cougar; if her artistic life has come before having kids, she is the "eccentric" (as in *strange*) maiden aunt.

As with all stereotypes, these popular depictions of childless elderwomen serve two functions: to dehumanize women whose lives have diverged from the norm, and, in doing so, to corral us into pursuing the ideal-normal of motherhood. As we have seen time and again, this "normal" forms the underpinnings of the gendered status quo.

And just as capitalism is predicated on the constant churn of the new, we are also quick to discard people, especially women, who have passed their sell-by date. Sometimes it feels like we're so addicted to novelty, so conditioned to go after shiny new things, that we just get *bored* of people who stick around too long.

And anyway, the sad reality is that grandmothers are also just as likely to be left to rot in nursing homes as older women without kids. In a society that views human beings as ultimately disposable, and which would rather not be reminded *that death is a natural part of life*, there is often no escaping being cast aside once one is seen as having surpassed one's usefulness. Meanwhile, the erasure of our elderwomen in general is part of what Sheehy describes as "a conspiracy of silence which has hidden the fact of *how much power* older women potentially wield." Power, remember, that lies partly in the fact that women over age fifty are no longer primarily caregivers and are therefore free to play more of an active role in society at large—and that is equally born from experience and the accumulation of common sense.

Once a person has taken a few turns around the block, it becomes much harder to hoodwink them into going against their own best interests. Having lived long enough to have overcome their fair share of traumas, and to have gotten the measure of how the world works, will also make a person far less likely to believe in the next quick fix or "miracle cure." They are more likely to retire their subscription to the capitalist credo of keeping up appearances and start living by their own playbook instead.

This is the essence of what it means to be sovereign: that is, the ultimate authority over our own life. When we are sovereign, we are no longer swayed by the projections and the expectations of others. As Jody Day describes it, "Being sovereign means you cannot be owned; that you are unownable." Meanwhile, age releases women from the belief that our value lies primarily in our physical attractiveness—or at least, the plump-faced, peachy-assed youthfulness that is symbolic of our fertility. In essence, this means being dis-*owned* by patriarchy—which in turn frees a woman to revalue herself on her own terms. To give far fewer fucks and to fully embody her *wise woman*; that is, the version of herself who trusts her lived experience above all else, and who, in doing so, might inspire others to do the same. Again, I believe *this is part of our collective legacy as women without kids.*

Having interviewed several childless elderwomen during the writing of this book, I have also been struck by the fact that they seemed to embody a certain ageless quality, the result, perhaps, of having deviated from the script that dictates what one should have achieved by when. Listening to them describe their lives, they seemed very much the same people in their seventies as they had been in their thirties. If anything, not having made the transition to motherhood meant never having to become somebody else—even if only until their kids were grown. As such, rather than a diminishing, it was as if the aging process brought a deepening and a ripening of the women they had always been. Contemplating this, I realized I'd always had the sense that I would become somehow *less* potent as I aged. But why wouldn't it be the same for me? *For us?*

Yes, bodies change, things stop functioning, and people get sick. But this can be the case at any stage of life; none of us is immune to the vulnerabilities of being human. And yes, a person's energy levels are going to ebb as the decades roll by. But by the law of physics, energy can never be created or destroyed; *it simply changes form*. If this is really true, then we can expect the energy and vitality that we embody at age thirty to be *different* to the energy we embody at age seventy, but not necessarily *diminished*. Especially if we haven't worn ourselves out busily fulfilling other people's expectations for our life. And for anybody who has spent their thirties, forties, and fifties developing an area of expertise or honing a craft, then who is to say that the transition to her wise-woman years won't simply bring a deeper, more confident settling into a vocation that she has come to wear like a second skin? The groove of her unique legacy having been carved more deeply into the edifice of her existence with each passing year.

This describes again the ripening that I picked up on when listening to women like Jeanne Safer and Marcia Drut-Davis (one of the first women to advocate for the choice to be childfree in the 1970s, and still active at age eighty), a sense of their essence having been condensed into something rich and delicious. And I can feel this same energy being exuded by the ranks of women-without-kids role models who have begun, slowly and surely, to populate my consciousness, like paper lanterns lighting the runway to my second adulthood.

Women like Bernardine Evaristo, who found global recognition at the age of sixty when she won the Booker Prize for *Girl, Woman, Other*, her ninth book. Like Stacey Abrams, balancing her political prowess with her creative life as an author. Like midlife icons Sarah Paulson, Naomie Harris, Marisa Tomei, and Tracee Ellis Ross. Like visionary film directors Kathryn Bigelow and Chloé Zhao, two of only three women to have won Oscars for their work at the time of writing—with Zhao's *Nomadland* depicting a bittersweet portrait of aging without kids. Like Danish author Karen Blixen, who defined "true piety"—true devotion to the life force energy that animates all things—as "loving one's destiny unconditionally." Or the poet Mary Oliver, who famously asked: "What is it you plan to do with your one wild and precious life?" Along with luminaries such as Oprah Winfrey, Gloria Steinem, and Stevie Nicks, these are the lives and the lived-in faces that I look to when I envision being nobody's grandma.

Each of these women, for me, seems both youthful and wise, experimental and accomplished, as if the little girl that she once was is right there, a twinkle in the corner of her own eye. Can you see her? But no woman without kids needs an Oscar to earn my admiration, or to prove her kick-ass crone credentials. All that is required to join this *unsung sisterhood* is for her to keep on being exactly who she is. To keep living and loving the life that is hers to live. For only when each and every one of us can wear the mantle proudly will we realize just how revolutionary it is to be women without kids.

Acknowledgments

THANKS MUST GO, first and foremost, to Mum and Dad, for deciding to embark on the unknowably challenging path of parenthood, and for never telling me what I ought to do with the life that you lavishly gifted me. Thank you also, parents, for reading this manuscript in its earlier stages and working with me to excavate the truth of our origin story.

Conversations with many women, with and without kids, helped me formulate the ideas and the arguments that I have presented here. In no particular order, for your time and your generous insights, thanks go to Kirsty Dare, Meena Ysanne, Sue Hunt, Diggy Lloyd, Jenna Good, Jessica Baum, Lucie Greene, Jody Day, Dr. Jeanne Safer, Orna Donath, Dr. Jennifer Mullen, Marine Sélénée, Aurelie Athan, Gillian Ragsdale, Justine Ang Fonte, adrienne maree brown, Rachel Diamond, Casey Aksoy, Dr. Nicole LePera, Zoë Noble, Claudia Boutote, Naama Simon, Holly Whitaker, Riane Eisler, Jenny Brown, Galit Atlas, Adama Sesay, Marcia Drut Davis, and Stacey London. Honorary mention to Carter Dillard. And a special thanks to all who responded to my *Women Without Kids* survey.

For your literary dissections of the parenthood prescription, thanks to Meghan Daum, Sheila Heti, Torrey Peters, Silvia Federici, Meg Mason, Lionel Shriver, Bernardine Evaristo, Inga Muscio, Meg Walitzer, Anna Solomon, and Emma Gannon. Posthumous thanks to Gail Sheehy and Adrienne Rich.

Coleen O'Shea, thanks for not running a mile when I told you I wanted to call my next book *Selfish Cunt*, and for helping it find its rightful home. Nina Renata Aron, thank you for helping me fine-tune my proposal (and for your mesmerizing writing on motherhood). Libby Edelson, without your wise eye and gimlet edits, this manuscript would be twice as long and largely indecipherable. Deep gratitude for your smarts and your treasured friendship.

On the team at Sounds True, thanks go to Diana Ventimiglia for saying an Affirmative Yes to this project; to Jaime Schwalb for helping me think bigger about my potential readership; to Laurel Szmyd, Leslie Brown, and Alan Getto for keeping things shipshape; to Sahar Al-Nima, Nick Small, and Chloe Prusiewicz for helping spread the word; and to Jeff Mack and Robbyn Kirylo for bringing me to Boulder to record the audiobook.

Lastly, thank you, S, for everything. It being just us has been just perfect.

Notes

1 statista.com/statistics/241535/percentage-of-childless--women-in-the-us-by-age/; cdc.gov/nchs/data/vsrr/vsrr012-508.pdf

2 healthdata.org/news-release/lancet-world-population-likely-shrink-after-mid-century-forecasting-major-shifts-global

3 theguardian.com/lifeandstyle/2021/jan/24/the-idea-of--having-a-baby-scares-me-what-if-my-child-is-horrible-mariella-frostrup

4 ecowatch.com/canada-ice-shelf-collapse-2646937803.html#:~:text=for the newsletter!-,Canada's Last Intact Ice Shelf the Size,Collapses Due to Global Warming&text=A 4%2C000%2Dyear%2Dold ice,intact ice shelves%2C Reuters reported

5 ihpi.umich.edu/news/forced-sterilization-policies-us-targeted-minorities-and-those-disabilities-and-lasted-21st#:~:text=State%2Dsanctioned sterilizations reached their,laws actually informed Nazi Germany

6 ccp.jhu.edu/2021/05/17/maternal-mortality
   -black-mamas-race-momnibus/?gclid=
   Cj0KCQjwuaiXBhCCARIsAKZLt3mQOJ
   _jPvqAz3adUiCh5KeZtJMlY3J4BMcUR6uoIrkyTi8ROX
   vPCf0aAtmoEALw_wcB

7 psychologytoday.com/us/blog/the-human-beast/201701
   /do-extraverts-have-more-children

8 forbes.com/sites/soulaimagourani/2019/11/24/what-does
   -having-a-real-family-mean/?sh=6bc8224e1871

9 criminaldefenselawyer.com/resources/criminal-defense
   /crime-penalties/marital-rape.htm

10 sciencedaily.com/releases/2011/11/111110142352.htm#:~:
   text=Summary%3A,about the mother's mental state

11 en.wikipedia.org/wiki/Phyllis_Schlafly#Equal_Rights
   _Amendment

12 cnbc.com/2021/03/24/equal-pay-day-single-moms-have
   -biggest-pay-gap.html

13 newportinstitute.com/resources/co-occurring-disorders
   /alcohol-abuse-in-women/

14 warren.senate.gov/newsroom/press-releases/warren-jones
   -and-colleagues-reintroduce-universal-child-care-and-early
   -learning-act-and-call-for-president-biden-to-invest-700
   -billion-in-child-care#:~:text=Establishes Universal Child
   Care without,%24700 billion over 10 years

15 parentingforbrain.com/childhood-emotional-neglect/

16 moneyandmentalhealth.org/financial-difficulties-suicide/#:
    ~:text=Our research found that people,payments over the
    same period

17 singlemotherguide.com/single-mother-statistics/

18 Orna Donath's term for an aspirational standard that is
    presented as attainable to all, but which actually only
    represents the lives and needs of a privileged few.

19 nautil.us/families-of-choice-are-remaking-america-rp-5257/

20 latimes.com/opinion/story/2021-11-28/1-in-4-adults-is
    -estranged-from-family-and-paying-a-psychological-price

21 ncbi.nlm.nih.gov/pmc/articles/PMC5548437/#:~:text=The
    second demographic transition entails,82%3B Lesthaeghe
    2010%2C pp

22 consumeraffairs.com/pets/pets-are-family.html

23 researchgate.net/publication/263928542-Childhood
    _Neglect_Attachment_to_Companion_Animals_Stuffed_
    Animals_As_Attachment_Objects_in_Women_and_Men

24 journals.sagepub.com/doi/full/10.1177
    /0265407518761225

25 ageuk.org.uk/latest-news/articles/2017/september/five
-million-grandparents-take-on-childcare-responsibilities
/; aarp.org/content/dam/aarp/research/surveys_statistics
/life-leisure/2019/aarp-grandparenting-study.doi.10
.26419-2Fres.00289.001.pdf

26 podcasts.apple.com/us/podcast/was-the-internet-a
-horrible-mistake/id1570872415?i=1000538441210

27 ifstudies.org/blog/the-conservative-fertility-advantage

28 podcasts.apple.com/us/podcast/nekkid-conversations
/id1519542577?i=1000491588060

29 Attachment issues and depression: link.springer.com
/article/10.1007/s10567-019-00299-9; attachment issues
and anxiety: psycnet.apa.org/record/2015-03786-004;
attachment issues and addiction: ncbi.nlm.nih.gov/pmc
/articles/PMC6803532/

30 businessinsider.com/amy-coney-barrett-asks-safe-haven
-laws-solutions-unwanted-motherhood-2021-12

31 Homelessness and foster care: nfyi.org/issues
/homelessness/; prison and foster care: clasp.org/blog
/young-leaders-advocate-ending-foster-care-prison
-pipeline/

32 npr.org/2020/03/18/817687042/deaths-of-despair
-examines-the-steady-erosion-of-u-s-working-class-life

33 en.wikipedia.org/wiki/The_Body_Keeps_the_Score

34 mkorostoff.github.io/1-pixel-wealth/

35 podcasts.apple.com/us/podcast/f-g-cancelled/
id1549437914?i=1000534636625

36 podcasts.apple.com/us/podcast/mark-wolynn-what-trauma
-have-you-inherited/id1282044290?i=1000447768156

37 centerforpartnership.org/programs/social-wealth-index/

38 cdn.simonssearchlight.org/wp-content/uploads/2020/08
/06100941/CHD2-brochure_Jan2020_final.pdf

39 publichealth.jhu.edu/2020/us-autism-rates-up-10-percent
-in-new-cdc-report

40 theatlantic.com/magazine/archive/2020/12/the-last
-children-of-down-syndrome/616928/

41 autismparentingmagazine.com/prenatal-test-autism/

42 amazon.com/Feminism-Politics-Resilience-Essays-Welfare/
dp/1509525076

43 en.wikipedia.org/wiki/The_Better_Angels_of_Our_Nature

44 vdoc.pub/documents/minimizing-marriage-marriage
-morality-and-the-law-726h4rv1q860

45 thetimes.co.uk/article/marian-keyes-on-her-life-lessons
-karma-is-codswallop-gr93mpl0c

46 theatlantic.com/family/archive/2021/08/why-parents-regret
-children/619931/

47 en.wikipedia.org/wiki/Erik_Erikson#Theories_of
_development_and_the_ego

48 theguardian.com/environment/2017/jul/12/want-to-fight
-climate-change-have-fewer-children

49 theguardian.com/commentisfree/2020/aug/26/panic--
overpopulation-climate-crisis-consumption-environment

50 A theory I learned about from Buddhist eco-chaplain
Lindsay Branham.

51 en.wikipedia.org/wiki/The_Denial_of_Death

52 forbes.com/sites/kathycaprino/2019/12/13/the-top-regrets
-of-the-dying-and-what-we-need-to-learn-from-them/?sh=
1b110e687ce7

About
Sounds True

SOUNDS TRUE was founded in 1985 by Tami Simon with a clear mission: to disseminate spiritual wisdom. Since starting out as a project with one woman and her tape recorder, we have grown into a multimedia publishing company with a catalog of more than 3,000 titles by some of the leading teachers and visionaries of our time, and an ever-expanding family of beloved customers from across the world.

In more than three decades of evolution, Sounds True has maintained our focus on our overriding purpose and mission: to wake up the world. We offer books, audio programs, online learning experiences, and in-person events to support your personal growth and awakening, and to unlock our greatest human capacities to love and serve.

At SoundsTrue.com you'll find a wealth of resources to enrich your journey, including our weekly *Insights at the Edge* podcast, free downloads, and information about our nonprofit Sounds True Foundation, where we strive to remove financial barriers to the materials we publish through scholarships and donations worldwide.

To learn more, please visit SoundsTrue.com/freegifts or call us toll-free at 800.333.9185.

Together, we can wake up the world.

sounds true
WAKING UP THE WORLD

About
the Author

RUBY WARRINGTON is a British-born author, editor, and publishing consultant. Recognized as having the unique ability to identify issues that are destined to become part of the cultural narrative, Ruby's other works include *Material Girl*, *Mystical World*, *Sober Curious*, and *The Sober Curious Reset*. Her work has been featured by countless media outlets globally, including the *New York Times*, CNN, *The Guardian*, and *Good Morning America*. She lives in Brooklyn.